Z   /i

kabbalah

Tradition of hidden knowledge

with 127 illustrations, 14 in colour

Thames and Hudson

To him who bears Thy Name

ART AND IMAGINATION
General Editor: Jill Purce

© 1979 Warren Kenton

Filmset in Great Britain by Keyspools Ltd,
Golborne, Lancashire.
Printed in the Netherlands

Contents

Preface

Rabbi Ishmael said: All the companions [the initiated] liken it to a man
who has a ladder in the midst of his
house whereby he can ascend and
descend without anyone to prevent
him. Blessed art Thou Lord God, Who
knowest all secrets and art the Lord of
hidden things.
Pirke Hekalot. Babylonia, 6th century.

Kabbalah is the inner and mystical aspect of Judaism. It is the perennial Teaching about the Attributes of the Divine, the nature of the universe and the destiny of man, in Judaic terms. Imparted by revelation, it has been handed down over the centuries by a discreet tradition that has periodically changed the mythological and metaphysical format to meet the spiritual and cultural needs of different places and epochs. This long and broadly spread history has given Kabbalah a remarkably rich and wide variety of images of reality which appear to the unversed eye as strange, obscure and even at times contradictory or corrupt. Therefore in this presentation one particular Kabbalistic system is used to unify and clarify a kaleidoscope of diverse views and practices drawn from ancient and modern sources. Finally it must be stated, in concordance with a strict Kabbalistic rule, that the exposition represents one man's comprehension of a living tradition as it exists in the world of today.

London, Autumn 1978/5738

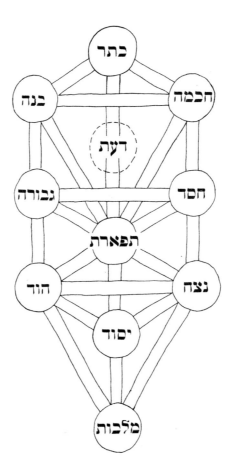

The Tree of Life

Manifestation

God is God. There is no thing to compare with God. God is God.

In Kabbalah, God the Transcendent is called AYIN. AYIN means in Hebrew 'No Thing', for God is beyond Existence. AYIN is neither below nor above; nor is it in movement or in stillness. There is nowhere AYIN is. God is Absolute Nothing.

AYIN SOF means 'Without End'. This is the title of God Who is everywhere. AYIN SOF is the One to the Zero of AYIN. This is the totality of what is and is not. AYIN SOF is God the Immanent, the Absolute All. AYIN SOF has no Attributes, because they can manifest only within existence, and existence is finite.

The oral tradition of Kabbalah states that the reason for existence is that 'God wished to behold God.' Thus there was a previous non-existence in which, as the written tradition says, 'Face did not gaze upon Face.' In an act of total free will, God withdrew the Absolute All, AYIN SOF, from one place to allow a void to appear in which the mirror of existence could be manifested. This act of Zimzum, contraction, lies behind the rabbinical saying, 'God's place is the world, but the world is not God's place.'

The divine act is visualized symbolically as follows. From AYIN SOF OR, the Endless Light that surrounds the void, there emanated a beam of light which penetrated from the periphery towards the centre. This, the Kav or beam of Divine Will, manifested in ten distinct stages of Emanation. This event is echoed in another rabbinical saying, that the world was called into being by ten Divine Utterances. Since the Middle Ages these ten stages have been known as the Sefirot. The word 'Sefirah' (the singular form) has no simple equivalent in any language, although its root relates it to the words 'cipher' (i.e. number) and 'sapphire'. Some have seen the Sefirot as Divine Powers or Vessels; others regard them as the instruments or tools of Divine Governance. Mystics have pictured them as the ten Faces, Hands or even Garments of God. All agree, however, that the Sefirot express Divine Attributes, which from the primal moment of Emanation are eternally held in a set of relationships until God wills them to vanish with the Void into Nothingness again.

The relationships between the Sefirot are governed by three unmanifest Divine principles, the 'Hidden Splendours' (Zahzahot) of Primordial Will, Mercy and Rigour (or Justice). Will holds the balance, while Mercy expands, and Rigour constrains, the flow of Emanation, and so they organize the ten Divine Attributes into a specific archetypal pattern. The pattern thus called forth is the model on which everything that is to come into manifestation is based. It has been named the Image of God, but it is more

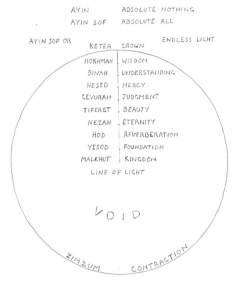

AYIN   ABSOLUTE NOTHING
AYIN SOF   ABSOLUTE ALL

AYIN SOF OR   ENDLESS LIGHT
KETER   CROWN

HOKHMAH   WISDOM
BINAH   UNDERSTANDING
HESED   MERCY
GEVURAH   JUDGMENT
TIFERET   BEAUTY
NEZAH   ETERNITY
HOD   REVERBERATION
YESOD   FOUNDATION
MALKHUT   KINGDOM

LINE OF LIGHT

VOID

ZIMZUM   CONTRACTION

The first manifestation

Ten Sefirot out of Nothing.
Ten not nine. Ten not eleven.
Understand this in Wisdom and in
Wisdom understand. Enquire and
ponder through their meaning, so as
to return The Creator to His Throne.
Sefer Yezirah. Babylonia, 6th century.

generally known as the Tree of Life. Each Sefirah in turn manifests under the influence of one of the Zahzahot in particular, and for this reason the flow which manifests the ten Sefirot can be visualized as zigzagging in a 'Lightning Flash' from a central position (Balance) to the right (Expansion) and across to the left (Constraint). Thus the Zahzahot give rise to the three vertical alignments in the Tree of Life diagram, known as the Pillars: that of Equilibrium (Grace, Will), in the centre, that of Mercy (active Force, Expansion) on the right, and that of Severity (passive Form, Constraint) on the left.

The relationships set forth in the Tree underlie the whole of existence; and so the properties of the Sefirot may be seen in terms of any branch of knowledge. Thus while their basic definition is as Attributes of God, they can be defined in terms of human experience because we too are cast in the Image of God. This anthropomorphic method is common in Kabbalah as elsewhere, and is freely applied as a symbolic language in metaphysical areas which pure abstractions cannot explain.

The first Sefirah, at the edge of the Void, is called in Hebrew Keter, the Crown. This manifestation contains all that was, is and will be; it is the place of first emanation and ultimate return. Its nature as a Divine Attribute is expressed by the Name of God which is traditionally attached to it: I AM THAT I AM. From this point of Equilibrium the beam of light expands, under the influence of Mercy, Force and Expansion, to manifest the second Sefirah, that of Hokhmah, Wisdom. This in the Divine and human minds is the active, inner intellect, experienced by human beings as the flash of genius, inspiration or revelation. It is balanced on the side of Severity, Form and Contraction by the third Sefirah, Binah, Understanding; this is intellect in its passive, receptive and reflective capacity. In human terms it manifests through reason and tradition.

After the beam has left Binah, which heads the Pillar of Severity, it touches the Pillar of Equilibrium below Keter, the Crown. This point of balance on the Tree is crucial; it is the place of Ruah ha Kodesh, the Holy Spirit, which hovers as a veil below the three 'supernal' Sefirot. It remains unmanifest, but it has a place within Manifestation, marked on the Tree by the 'non-Sefirah' of Daat, Knowledge. This, we are told, is where the Absolute may enter at will to intervene directly in existence, which is now eternally held until Divine Will allows it to vanish like the image it is. In human terms Daat is the Knowledge that emerges out of nowhere and comes direct from God. It is quite different from the revelation of Wisdom (Hokhmah); Daat is not only seen but known. It is different, too, from what comes of Understanding (Binah) or deep pondering: Daat, the child of the supernal Sefirot, is not only observation but becoming.

Below Daat the Flash passes to the Pillar of Mercy (Expansion) and back to the Pillar of Severity (Contraction), and a pair of Sefirot are defined which govern the level of emotion as distinct from supernal intellect. The Attribute of active or inner emotion is Hesed, Mercy; that of passive or outer emotion is Gevurah, Justice. Both Sefirot have other Hebrew names and other translated equivalents, but all are inadequate to explain the Attributes; those used here merely approximate to the active and passive Divine principles involved. In ourselves these qualities appear in complementary

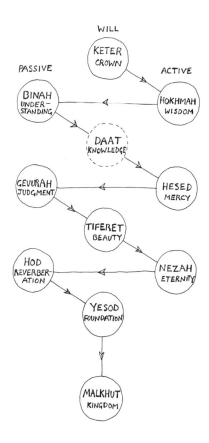

The Lightning Flash

tendencies towards love, tolerance and generosity on the one hand (Hesed) and discipline, rigour and discrimination on the other (Gevurah). At this, the emotional level, the operation of opposing Sefirotic principles, and the dangers of going too far in one direction or the other, become part of everyday experience: Justice and Mercy underlie every human transaction, from a summit conference to the choice of a birthday present.

The Lightning Flash, having passed from the expansive principle of Hesed to the constrictive principle of Gevurah, now returns, a stage lower, to the Pillar of Equilibrium. Here is manifested the central Sefirah of Tiferet, Beauty or Adornment. This lies at the heart of the Tree, relating directly to all the Sefirot of the Pillars of Severity and Mercy. Whenever the Tree diagram is applied – as it can be – to the dynamics of any organism or system, Tiferet is where the essence of the thing can be found. On the Divine Tree, Tiferet is the Heart of Hearts. With the emotional Sefirot of Hesed and Gevurah it forms the triad of the Divine soul; with the higher Sefirot of Hokhmah and Binah it forms the great triad of the Divine spirit, in the midst of which hovers the Ruah ha Kodesh. In the human psyche Tiferet is the Self, the core of the individual, which lies behind the everyday ego: the 'Watcher' which focuses the largely unconscious influences of the higher centres of Mercy and Justice (Hesed and Gevurah), Wisdom and Understanding (Hokhmah and Binah).

Below Tiferet the Lightning Flash manifests two more complementary Attributes, the lowest on the Pillars of Mercy and Severity. On the active, expansive side is Nezah, Eternity, and on the passive, constrictive side is Hod, Reverberation. Traditionally the Hebrew names of these Attributes were translated as Victory and Splendour; but their operation as Sefirot is better expressed by the names used here, which correspond equally well to the Hebrew roots. They belong to the operative, instrumental level of action in the structure of the Tree; they traditionally correspond in Divine terms to the (expansive and constrictive) roles of the Hosts of God, sent out to do the Divine Will. In human terms they represent the vital psycho-biological processes, whether active, instinctive and impulsive (Nezah, Eternity) or passive, cognitive and controlling (Hod, Reverberation).

On the Pillar of Equilibrium, between and below these two practical Sefirot, is Yesod, Foundation. Like every Sefirah in the sequence, it contains all that has gone before; and therefore it is a complex Attribute with many qualities. First, it is generative: it is from this point, as will be seen, that further Trees manifest. Second, it is reflective: here, directly below Tiferet, an 'image of the image' can be perceived, and the Tree sees itself; Yesod is the mirror within the Mirror. These two complementary functions mean that its constitution (or Foundation) must be clear and sound; hence the inner meaning of sexual purity associated with this Sefirah. In ourselves it appears as the ego, the lower place of consciousness, in which we see ourselves, and which projects a persona for others to see which may or may not (according to our state of balance and self knowledge) reflect the true nature of the self at Tiferet. Most of our perception of the world, and most of our implementation of Will, takes place at Yesod.

The lowest Sefirah, the complement to Keter the Crown, is Malkhut, the Kingdom. In it the Divine Lightning Flash is earthed. It constitutes the

Shekhinah, the Presence of God in matter. Its nature is fourfold, encapsulating the four levels inherent within the Tree as a whole (the root, trunk, branch and fruit of the Tree as it grows down into existence; or the Will, Mind, Heart and Body of the Divine). In ourselves the four levels of Malkhut appear as the body, with its traditional four elements, earth, water, air and fire: the solids, liquids, gases and radiations whose interactions keep us alive.

We now have the general scheme of the Sefirot. Three are aligned on the active right-hand Pillar of Mercy, three on the passive left-hand Pillar of Severity, and four (plus the non-Sefirah, Daat) on the central Pillar of Equilibrium or Grace. Their relationships, established by the Lightning Flash, are further realized by a total of twenty-two paths, which in turn form a system of triangular configurations or triads, active on the right and passive on the left; the horizontal and central triads, linking all three Pillars, are concerned directly with consciousness. The scheme is set out on p. 40.

Out of all the foregoing comes a most subtle metaphysical and mythological configuration. It has been taken many stages further in the study of various constellations of Sefirot, and of the minute dynamics within each Sefirah as mutually imparted and reflected flows move along the paths to act upon the miniature Tree which constitutes each Sefirah.

Four Worlds

The Tree of Life as it first comes into existence constitutes a Divine World of Emanation (Azilut, Proximity, in Hebrew): a perfect configuration of Divine Attributes. All the dynamics and laws inherent in the World of Azilut are complete, except that nothing has happened, and nothing will happen, unless there is movement in time and space. Neither yet exists, because Azilut is still at the stage of pure Will. It could have remained alone in this pristine condition throughout Eternity, had not God willed the beginning of Days, the unfolding of Creation in a sequence of great cosmic cycles or Ages (Shemittot) in which the Divine Presence would manifest in space from the highest firmament to the minutest particle, and in time from Eternity to the smallest instant of Now as it moves through the Week of Ages towards the End of Days when everything will be complete. All this huge movement begins within Azilut and operates according to the laws generated by the Sefirot.

In Isaiah 43:7 are the words: 'Even every one that is called by My Name; for I have created him for My Glory, I have formed him: yea I have made him.' These four levels of calling, creating, forming and making recur throughout the Scriptures and throughout Kabbalah. They exist within the primordial Tree of Life, in Azilut (see p. 40), and correspond symbolically to its root, trunk, branch and fruit, or to the four letters of the Tetragrammaton or most special Name of God, YHVH. They are also perceived, for example, in the familiar four elements of the lowest Sefirah, Malkhut. As such they represent four levels or stages of removal from the source of All. The first level, associated with fire, is closest to the Crown (Keter) and is seen as symbolic of pure Will (the Divine 'calling'). The second, associated with air, is symbolic of Intellect (the Divine 'creation'). The third level, associated with water, is seen as an expression of Emotion, in ever changing forms (the Divine 'forming'). The fourth and last, associated with earth, speaks of Action, the practical implementation of all that has gone before (the Divine 'making'). Each level contains the qualities and activities of the one above, so that each descending level in turn is under more laws, is more complex, and is further from the source.

Although perfect, Azilut is not in itself fully realized: it is like the will to have a house which has been conceived but not yet defined in principle, designed in form, and built – and which nevertheless contains the germ of all these processes. Likewise these four levels inherent in Azilut unfold themselves in four great stages, each a World in itself, in the following way. Conceived in Azilut (fire), Manifestation calls forth in principle (air) the cosmic process of Creation (Beriah in Hebrew), which can be understood in terms of a second complete Tree emerging from the first. From Beriah there emerges a third, fluid World of Formation (Yezirah), from which a fourth, solid World of Action (Asiyyah) comes into existence. Each level has its own Tree, each World following in its own context the exact configuration and dynamics of the Tree of Azilut, and each therefore having within its reality the same four levels.

The origin of this conception, and of the understanding of the dynamics of the relationship between one World and the next, lies in the Hebrew text of the Bible. The Divine 'calling by My Name' which is the essence of Azilut means that each Sefirah has attached to it one of the Names of God. Keter, the Crown, has the Name EHYEH ASHER EHYEH, I AM THAT I AM: the beginning and end of all Existence. The Sefirot of Wisdom and Understanding, Hokhmah and Binah, have been given the names YHVH and ELOHIM respectively, which ancient belief associates with the Merciful and Just aspects of the Deity. At Tiferet, which is the focus of the Paths from these three Sefirot, is God the Creator, known by the composite Name of YHVH ELOHIM. The rest of the Sefirot have Divine Names of their own, and are understood by some Kabbalists to be the ELOHIM referred to collectively in the opening sentence of Genesis, *Berashith bara ELOHIM*, 'In the beginning the ELOHIM created'. The word ELOHIM is plural, and thus the creative process begins as the different Attributes of God, embodied in the Divine Names, will Creation to be called forth.

The first chapter of Genesis should be understood as the unfolding of Creation *from an already existing Divine World*. While this is common knowledge in Jewish esoteric cosmogony, it is still not known to many people familiar with the Bible. This concept disposes of the countless arguments that have gone on over the centuries as to whether Creation was brought forth out of nothing (*ex nihilo*), all of which rest on an ignorance of the previous existence of Divine Emanation (Azilut). This notion of pre-existence is alluded to, for instance, in the direct assertion in rabbinical tradition that God consulted the Torah (the Teaching) before the Universe was created, formed and made.

Creation in this particular Kabbalistic scheme begins in being willed or called forth by I AM THAT I AM. This Calling manifests at the heart of the Azilutic Tree, Tiferet, where God the Creator creates, forms and makes from

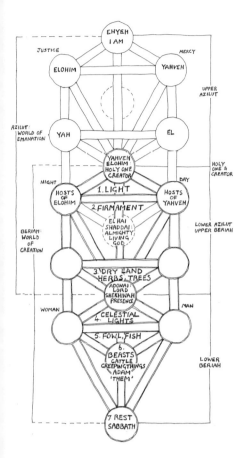

Azilut and Beriah: Emanation
brings forth Creation

*Thou wast the same before the
universe was created;
Thou hast been the same since the
universe hath been created;
Thou art the same in this universe,
and Thou wilt be the same in the
universe to come.
Jewish morning prayer.*

the three lowest levels of Azilut a new Tree and a new World. This World of Beriah is unfolded biblically in terms of the seven Days of Creation. The first Day saw the ordering of the chaotic Force and Form of Creation by the emergence of Light and Dark, that is the Pillars of Mercy and Justice, implemented by God the Creator operating from what was to be Keter, the Crown of the new Tree. This is the supernal triad of the Tree of Creation. On the second Day, the Azilutic triad of Nezah, Hod and Malkhut becomes the upper great triad of the Tree of Beriah: a Creative Wisdom, Understanding and Beauty, Hokhmah, Binah and Tiferet. This process is spoken of in Genesis as the dividing of the firmament between the waters above and those below, that is the parting from the Divine of what is to be called a separated World. The next five Days are a step-by-step unfolding of the Tree of Creation, with each level precisely related to a set of Sefirot, until on the last Day the Creator comes to rest in the lowest Beriatic Sefirah, that of the Kingdom (Malkhut), thus completing the Work, which 'was very good'. This comment is no mere self-congratulation: it hints at the several previous attempts at making a balanced Universe which are referred to in the Jewish esoteric tradition. Kabbalists call these the 'Kings of Edom', who reigned according to the Bible 'before there were Kings in Israel'. The reason for their failure, we are told, was an excess of one Pillar or one Sefirah. The Creation in Genesis was balanced, therefore good.

In the second chapter of Genesis the whole process seems to be repeated; some scholars consider this a scribal licence, but to the Kabbalist it is obviously not so, because of a crucial word change. Verse 1:27 says: 'So God created man', *Vayivra ELOHIM et ha Adam*. That is, the ELOHIM created Adam. At 2:7 the text says: *YHVH ELOHIM vayitzer et ha Adam*, 'and the Lord God formed man'. Between the words 'created' and 'formed' there is literally a World of difference, in that this second chapter is concerned with another and more fully worked out Sefirotic Tree which has come to be called Olam ha Yezirah, the World of Formation. The quality of this World is that of ever-changing phenomena, as it is worked upon by the dynamics of Creation and Divine Will above. It can be compared to the design phase in which an idea, which the architect has willed (Azilut) and creatively defined (Beriah), takes detailed form before its actual construction. Yezirah is a realm of differentiation and complication; it is the level on which, for example, the Beriatic spirit of the horse or the dog, that is the creature which has its origin in the World of Creation, undergoes endless modification into types and individual forms. The World of Yezirah was the Garden of Eden where the androgynous man created in Beriah (Genesis 1:27) was separated into Adam and Eve in clearly differentiated male and female reflections of the outer Pillars.

The fourth World, Asiyyah, emerges in its turn out of the one above. Genesis speaks of it in the reference to the river which flowed out of Eden, and which had four heads: a repetition of the four levels inherent in the Tree of Life, and in each separated World. This lowest World of Making, or of Elements and Action, is the World into which we ourselves, as Adam and Eve, have descended. It is manifest in the universe that we experience through our senses, with its (apparent) solidity and its liquid, gaseous and radiant aspects. To the scientist this material World has energy and matter:

10

that is, the qualities of the right and left Pillars of Force and Form. Those aware of more than the interaction of phenomena under natural law see it as the physical overlay to subtler and higher Worlds that permeate the whole of existence. Some physicists, indeed, have suspected that beyond the subatomic scale, as beyond the most distant galaxy, there is another kind of universe that seems somehow to be present within the very fabric of this, perhaps not so solid, scientific cosmos. Thus even at the most mundane level there is a consciousness of other dimensions that contain and influence the natural world and permeate it with a supernatural reality.

The Four Worlds interpenetrate the whole of existence. Schematically they may be seen as a 'Jacob's Ladder', with the Tree of one World growing out of the structure of the last, so that the Will of God, and the flow which connects all that exists, is present in everything that is manifest. In each case the Foundation (Yesod) of the higher World underlies the lower World as its Daat. In this particular scheme it will be noted that the sequence of Sefirot also unfolds down the axis, so that the long line or Kav of Divine Will runs throughout all the Worlds. The Four Worlds have been visualized in many ways – ranging from concentric geometries to anthropomorphic likenesses of Adam, or a succession of Halls or Sacred Hill of gardens. However, it must be remembered that no image can capture the reality, any more than a portrait, however deep or brilliant, can catch more than an aspect of a person. Kabbalah has constantly changed the *forms* in which it expresses a single all-embracing conception of reality; the intention is that no picture of existence shall become a fixed image that might be considered the ultimate. Alas, orthodoxy has never understood this principle and often takes authority from redundant formulations.

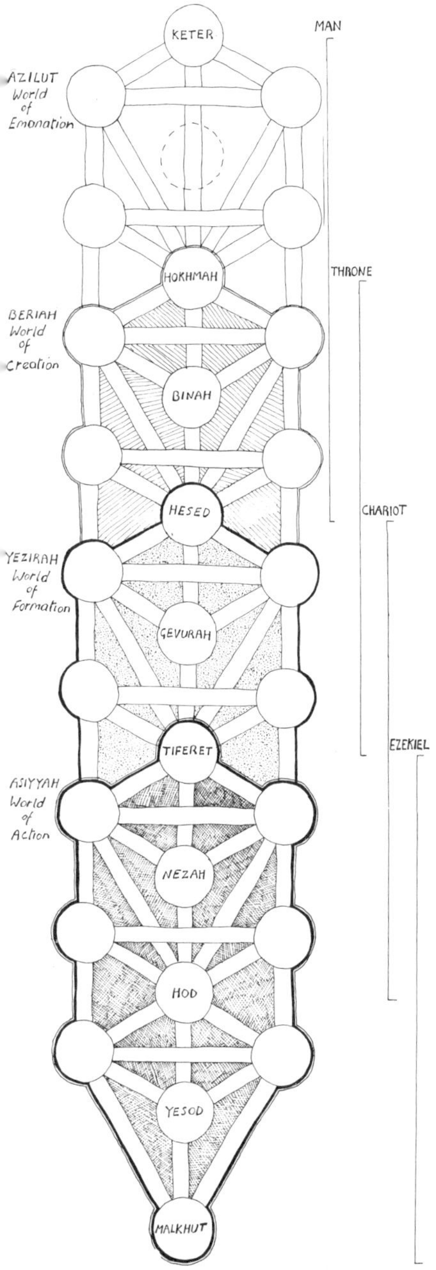

KETER
AZILUT
World of Emanation
HOKHMAH
BERIAH
World of Creation
BINAH
HESED
YEZIRAH
World of Formation
GEVURAH
TIFERET
ASIYYAH
World of Action
NEZAH
HOD
YESOD
MALKHUT
MAN
THRONE
CHARIOT
EZEKIEL

The four Worlds and Ezekiel's vision

As to the inhabitants of the Worlds, little need be said about the Tachutonim, those who 'dwell here below' in Asiyyah or the natural realm: we see them about us, while remaining largely unconscious of our own part in the higher Worlds. As for the Elyonim, those who 'dwell above', they are not perceptible through the ordinary senses; but it is logical to suppose – if one has ever experienced supernatural intervention – that the upper Worlds are peopled by inhabitants confined to other realities. These creatures are visualized in the Kabbalistic scheme as angels and archangels, or the 'fish' and 'fowl' (Genesis 1:26) who swim in the waters of the Yeziratic World of Formation and fly in the air of the Beriatic World of Creation. Such creatures have their part in the grand design of existence, and while we may not directly perceive their cosmic operations, we are certainly affected by them, as natural rhythms, planetary cycles and stellar variations affect terrestrial conditions to create changing climates, epochs of outer history and periods of human spirituality and inner progress.

To complete the cosmic picture, there is in Kabbalah a concept known as Kelippot or the World of Shells. This is the recognition of the demonic or destructive forces present in the created universe. According to tradition, the remnants of the previous Worlds that were discarded by the Creator still exist. Their task, at both the macrocosmic and microcosmic levels, is to intervene in order to test goodness and prove it sound. These demonic forces appear to be evil, but, as is observed in the book of Job, Satan the tester is one of the Sons of God. It is as cosmic functionaries that the forces of Chaos seek to disrupt the balance of the universe at the level of the three lower Worlds and to feed off what has not been made whole. These demonic creatures or Sheddim constitute a formidable opposition to mankind, which is particularly susceptible to their influence. The reason for this is that Adam, as the image of God, possesses free will and choice. He manifests the issue of good and evil, along with all the other privileges and duties of a human being.

Adam

Down the centuries the Divine World of Azilut has been called by many titles and described in many ways. Some rabbis have seen it as the Garment of Light that God wraps about the Divine Presence; some have symbolized it in the Shem ha Meforash, the most special Name of God, represented by the four letters YHVH. It has been called the Glory of God, and at one point in Kabbalistic history it was cast in the image of a great and radiant human figure called the Kabod. This Divine Man appears in the vision of the prophet Ezekiel who saw the Four Worlds as the likeness of a man (Azilut) seated on a heavenly throne (Beriah) which was set on a chariot (Yezirah) which in turn moved above the earth (Asiyyah).

The primordial Azilutic Man, called forth (as are we) in the configuration of the ten Sefirot, was thus an Adam before the Adam of Genesis was created and formed: his name is Adam Kadmon. He is the first of four reflections of God to become manifest as existence extends from Divinity to Materiality, before returning to merge again at the end of Time. Conceived in human shape, Adam Kadmon contains everything that is needed to complete the task of Divine reflection. He is both the mirror and the viewer, and has within his being will, intellect, emotion and capacity for action. Most of all, Adam Kadmon is conscious of the Divine, although at the moment of his calling forth his state is an innocent awareness of it, as a fish is oblivious of the sea in which it exists. Only after a descent through all the Worlds will he come to know in experience all the aspects of Divinity, perceiving in himself and in the universe the Face of God; this reflection, however, like that in any mirror, is only an image and never the reality. Direct contact comes only by way of Grace, or on the Completion of the entire cycle, both out into Manifestation and back to its source through Teshuvah or redemption.

The composition of Adam Kadmon is based on the Sefirot. Whereas the Tree of Life grows downwards from the Crown, Adam Kadmon stands on his feet (p. 68). Above his head is Keter, the Crown, while the two side Sefirot of Wisdom and Understanding, Hokhmah and Binah, relate to the hemispheres of his brain. The non-Sefirah of Knowledge, Daat, sits over his face and throat, for here he sees, hears, smells and speaks. The Sefirot of the heart, Gevurah and Hesed, the just and the merciful, are placed to left and right of his chest; while the central Sefirah, Tiferet or the self, is located over his solar plexus. The two lower and outer functional Sefirot, Hod and Nezah, are associated with the legs, and Yesod, the generative Foundation, with the genitals; Malkhut the Kingdom is at his feet. He is usually, although not always, depicted from the back, as Moses saw the Divine image (Exodus 33:20: 'For there shall no man see [My face] and live'), and so the active and passive sides are in their natural positions to right and left of the central Pillar of the spine.

References to this vast Divine figure are found in several early Kabbalistic works; and some literal-minded people have been offended by the detailed accounts of faces, beards and limbs which suggest that God's stature might be measured. In reality, the symbol of Adam Kadmon, like many others, is no more than an analogue, in metaphoric form, of the laws expressed in the arrangement of the Divine Attributes. Many other traditions have considered Man as the image of God to be the perfect model through which to study the Divine. Kabbalists are no exception and follow the esoteric maxim, 'As above, so below' in their study of the macrocosm and the microcosm.

Out of the Divine Man Adam Kadmon, as out of Azilut, comes the Beriatic Adam who was created on the sixth Day, when the action was focused upon the Yesod or Foundation of the Tree of Creation (see p. 10). Jewish legend has it that this Beriatic Adam was created last of all the creatures so that he would be humble; the Kabbalistic view is that all other creatures without exception – even the angels and archangels – are based on the Adam of Azilut but were left incomplete: only the Beriatic Adam was a complete image of the Divine. This fact accounts for the myth of jealousy and discord among the angelic hosts; those who would not concede human superiority, such as Lucifer, were relegated to the task of leading the chaotic forces that plague the universe and man in particular. The rebellion in Creation, even before Adam's fall, occurred because Creation, being the first of the separated Worlds, at one remove from the Divine, was initially allowed a small measure of free will in its inhabitants. This inherent risk of deviation from the cosmic plan was corrected, legend tells us, by the attachment of the Divine Name EL to the functional name of each angelic being, so that it could never exert more of its power than God wished. Thus each celestial being was confined to its task, like the angel Shalgiel who dealt only with snow.

Adam in Beriah, now existing as a separated entity on the level of the spirit, was still untried, and so the manifestation of God's image was brought forth into the third World of Formation, Yezirah, Eden. Here, the now divided but related aspects of male and female took up the active and passive roles (or, as some Kabbalists see it, the inner relationship of Adam the spirit to the soul of Eve). With the intrusion of temptation into their idyllic world came the wilful breaking of the one rule they had been given. With this came Knowledge of the World of Creation and the possibility of eating of the Tree of Life, that is Azilut; and so they were sent down into the lowest World of materiality and given coats of skins (Genesis 3:21), that is, fleshly bodies. Here they were placed under the greatest number of laws, so that the universe was relatively safe from the results of their free will until they had matured into greater responsibility. In mythological form, this is an account of how we arrived on the earth. Some Kabbalists see this event of the Fall as foreseen by God, as a parent lets a child make a mistake in order to learn. In this manner Adam experiences all the levels of existence, both on the way

Man contains all that is above in heaven and below upon earth, the celestial as well as the terrestrial creatures; it is for this reason that the Ancient of Ancients chose Man as His Divine manifestation. No World could exist before Adam came into being, for the human figure contains all things, and all that is exists by virtue of it. Zohar. Spain, 13th century.

13

down and on the way up as he seeks to regain first Eden, then the Heaven of Creation and ultimately Union with the Divine.

Kabbalistic tradition, viewing the situation from below, goes into much detail concerning our origins and incarnation as individuals. It says that each one of us was present in the Azilutic body of Adam Kadmon, and that we were therefore in existence before Creation began; Creation was to be the setting for our individual destiny. When the four Worlds were complete and operational, the Divine part of each human entity became differentiated into cells within the being of the Created (Beriatic) Adam. Here, in the realm of pure spirit, we resided in innocence until we were sent down into the treasure-house of souls in Paradise where the Beriatic, differentiated part of our nature, which enclosed the Divine spark of Azilut, took on a Yeziratic form while waiting for the correct time to go down and be incarnated in the physical universe of Asiyyah. When that moment came we were called before the Most High, Who told us of our particular task and the gifts we had received in order to carry it out. This is our destiny, although apparently there is much reluctance to descend into what one Kabbalist called this 'vale of tears'. The answer always is, 'It was for this you were called, created, formed and made.'

One tradition tells us further that when a couple are in sexual union the invisible presence of their child hovers above them, and that when conception occurs the Beriatic body, or spirit, and the Yeziratic body, or soul, become attached to the embryonic Asiyyatic body of this world. As the foetus grows, so the person to be incarnated becomes involved in acquiring a coat of skin. Detailed accounts add that during this time of physical gestation the person is shown his forthcoming life, the people he will meet and the places he will go. He also glimpses the results of other people's lives after death, and the levels to which they might individually ascend or descend according to their performance, so that he is no longer in a state of innocence but begins the process of experience as he passes via gestation into incarnation. When the child is born the prenatal process is cut off, and the person begins to forget his memories of the upper Worlds as he becomes increasingly involved in the physical life of being a baby. From time to time, however, he will faintly recall a prenatal moment, and later even dimly recognize a scene or individual he was shown before birth. The people he will meet are likewise involved in the cosmic plan and have also their destinies and fates to live out, so that, when two people meet who have already been acquainted prior to life, there is a strange familiarity.

Having been born into the natural realm, and coming under such laws as being composed of mineral matter, feeding and propagating like a vegetable, and moving and relating to others like an animal, it can be said that the person has now personally descended through all four Worlds. However, as he grows into maturity, passing up through the various stages of life, it may be seen that he also begins his ascent back into the upper Worlds. This rising process follows the Lightning Flash in reverse, so that he develops first of all his body or Malkhut, in foetal growth; then his ego-mind or Yesod, in babyhood; then his capacity to learn or Hod, in childhood; and then his Nezah, which relates to the active and instinctual preoccupations of youth.

On reaching the Tiferet stage of self awareness – the prime of life – he may, by choice, stop and develop no more, and merely spend the rest of his life repeating or cultivating the strengths and weaknesses of the lower Sefirot, to become totally preoccupied with Malkhutian materialism, Yesodic egoism, the clever games of Hod, or the sensual pleasures of Nezah. In the case of a person who does develop some self will or Tiferet power, he may become a dominant and even great (but natural) individual, an 'animal man', concerned with ruling others with good or ill will. Such people are found among politicians, and indeed in any profession of influence from science to the arts and industry. Here, again, an individual may remain for a lifetime until his power abates and his place is taken by another natural king or queen. Only those people who see life as more than comfort, power and status may go on to perceive the inner and upper connections with the superior Worlds. This stage, however, requires more than desire for, or even glimpses of, that other reality. It needs to begin with self knowledge; and here we come to Kabbalah's view of the anatomy of the psyche.

Anatomy

Yezirah and Asiyyah: mind and body

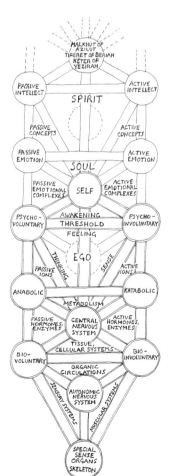

We have seen how ancient Kabbalists have related an anthropomorphic scheme to the Sefirotic Tree, in that Adam Kadmon has an anatomy of Will, Intellect, Emotion and Action. This model is extended down through the Four Worlds, each World representing the cosmic manifestation of one of these same levels. In the microcosm of an individual incarnate human being the scheme is repeated in miniature.

Kabbalists down the ages have always set out their comprehension of these eternal principles in the language of their own time. This is observed, for instance, in the symbolic psychology of the Zohar or Book of Splendour, written in medieval Spain, and in the detailed analysis of the various levels of a man by the Hasidic Habad school in eighteenth-century Russia. Modern Kabbalists continue the tradition, and set out their knowledge in the psychological terms of our own time. This is how a tradition continues to live.

Beginning with the lowest World, let us look at the body. This physical vehicle, which has evolved over millions of years, is based upon a distinct set of principles which, while related to earthly conditions, are also rooted in the archetypal laws that govern existence, namely the Sefirot. Thus at its most elementary level the body operates upon the interaction of earth, water, air and fire. This can be observed in such structures and systems as the bones and muscles, the chemical interflows, the gaseous exchanges and electronic activity. In greater detail the hierarchy of mechanical organic tissues, metabolic and electromagnetic systems, can be seen as the interaction of the Pillars of Force and Form, energy and matter, as the active and passive sides of the Tree work under the direction of the will of the senses at Malkhut, the autonomic nervous system at Yesod or Foundation, and the central nervous system, including the brain, at Tiferet, the Seat of

Solomon. Thus energy and matter are bound during the life of the body to the will and consciousness inherent in the central Pillar. The upper face of the Asiyyatic Tree is the subtle part of the body and represents what is called in Kabbalah the Zelim or image, which corresponds to the etheric connection between body and psyche. Partly physical, it is composed of the finest energy and matter found in the lowest World and corresponds with the coarsest of the next World, with whose lower half (or lower face) it interpenetrates. Some people can perceive this level with the inner eye and see its radiant aura surrounding the body. The Keter, or Crown, of the body Tree matches in this Kabbalistic scheme the Tiferet of the Yeziratic, Formative World of the soul or psyche and the Malkhut of the Beriatic, Creative World of the spirit. This shows how the three lower Worlds meet in those living in the flesh, and how it is possible to experience the unseen Worlds at moments when we perceive a deeper reality behind the face of the physical World.

The anatomy of the psyche is based upon the same Sefirotic model as that of the body; but its energy, substance and consciousness are those of the subtle World of Formation. To be exact, the only direct contact with the physical World is through the elemental Malkhut of the Yeziratic Tree, which relates to the Tiferet of the body, that is the brain and central nervous system. This demonstrates the accuracy of this scheme of interpenetrating Worlds, as it is here that the brain, the physical organ of cognition, fuses consciousness with tissue, metabolism and electro-magnetic fields. Directly above is the non-Sefirah of Daat or Knowledge of the body, which corresponds with the Yesod or Foundation of the psyche. In this way the two Worlds meet and interact, the lower in supplying data about the exterior World, and the upper in perceiving it psychologically as well as transmitting to the body, and to the world outside, the Will descending from the inner and upper realms.

The Yesod of the psyche, the ordinary ego-mind, is the level of consciousness, part physical and part psychological, that forms the Foundation of what we think, feel and do. Indeed, this is borne out in the configuration of the Tree by the triangular patterns or triads that surround Yesod; these are defined by the three paths flowing in from Malkhut, Hod and Nezah (see p. 40), the angles of what is called the vegetable triad of the psyche. By this is meant all the routine processes of action, feeling and thought that go to make up the everyday activity of life. Thus it will be seen that the triad on the left has the passive, reflective quality of thinking, the one on the right or active side that of action, while the central horizontal triad above the ego, with the dual nature of being active or passive, has the introverted quality of feeling. A little personal observation of the ego's changing state demonstrates the veracity of the scheme. For example, while one may *feel* depressed as one *thinks* about a problem it is still possible to *do* one's work.

The vegetable state of the ego may be influenced by events deep in the psyche, but its view of the world is primarily formed by what it has imbibed from education and upbringing. Thus a city-bred person exhibits many differences from a country-born individual in attitude and values at the ordinary vegetable level of life. Together with Hod and Nezah – the psycho-

'And God created man in His image.' It is this image which receives us first when we come into this World, it develops with us while we grow and accompanies us when we leave the earth. Its source is in heaven. Zohar. Spain, 13th century.

biological Sefirot of control and desire which define the frontier or threshold of everyday consciousness – and Malkhut the body connection, Yesod the ego makes this lower great triangle with its three sub-divisions the chief area of experience for most people. Yesod moreover focuses the image a person has of himself, be it scholar, cowboy or housewife.

The next triad, composed of the Yeziratic Hod, Nezah and Tiferet, forms the zone just beyond what is called the normal liminal line of consciousness. Set between Hod and Nezah, which balance and power the bio-psychological processes, and reaching beyond to Tiferet the self or inner Watcher, this triad is named the animal or awakening threshold. Here, when the power of Nezah is aroused and the sensitivity of Hod is alerted, a heightened awareness occurs that is sometimes experienced in moments of profound peace or great drama. This is the place of the first ecstasy, sudden lucidity, deep passion and partial illumination. This is quite different from ordinary ego consciousness, and can lead to a state beyond even the animal condition of directed will into the recognition of Worlds above the physical – and even beyond the psychological, because the self is not only the Crown (Keter) of the body and the core (Tiferet) of the psyche but the elemental base (Malkhut) of the spirit.

Experience of this level is not uncommon, although it operates most often from the unconscious, that is across the Hod-Nezah threshold that divides the self from the ego. The path that joins Tiferet and Yesod, across this threshold, is called by some Kabbalists the path of the Zadek or Honest Man; but it becomes this only when it is clear of self-deception and psychological laziness.

The self resides in the Seat of Solomon of the psyche. This is that part of us that observes all. Having paths flow into it from above and below, it is the centre of a series of triads formed by the upper as well as the lower Sefirot. As will be seen, the passive and active Sefirot of intellect (Binah and Hokhmah) and emotion (Gevurah and Hesed) work off their respective Pillars and not only relate to each other via the paths, but focus on Tiferet. The triads on the left are the passive emotional and intellectual banks of complexes and concepts that hold the psyche in check, while those on the right are active and stimulate emotional and intellectual activity. On the Tree of the psyche the side triads complement each other, as they store ideas and emotions and continually adjust the inner balance of the individual as he progresses through life.

The horizontal triad above the self is the level of soul. Composed of Gevurah, Hesed and Tiferet – the emotional Sefirot of Justice and Mercy and the Sefirah of the self – it is the place of self consciousness and conscience. It is here, in what has traditionally been called the moral triad, that the individual perceives his own and others' ethical performance and metes out justice and mercy. According to an ancient view, this is the place where one's good and bad angels reside to tempt and encourage. Here, too, is found the gateway to Paradise and Purgatory. These archetypal symbols describe states of the soul, and anyone operating at this level of self awareness knows its criteria are not of the natural world. Real morality is not the same as social or tribal custom. The soul is deep within the normally unconscious levels of the psyche, and is intimately associated with the side

One man is equivalent to all Creation. One man is a World in miniature. Abot de Rabbi Nathan. Palestine,2nd century.

17

triads of emotions and concepts. It also has access, via the self at Tiferet, to the spirit, the great upper triad of Hokhmah, Binah, Tiferet.

The triad of the spirit is made up of the Sefirot of Wisdom and Understanding and the self, with psychological Knowledge at its centre. This triad, it will be realized, is also the lower triad of the World of Creation above. Thus, on the Yeziratic side, it is the spiritual aspect of the psyche, where the individuality of the self, as expressed in the soul, is seen within a cosmic context. The lower face of the Yeziratic Tree – its physical aspect culminating in Tiferet – is, it will be seen, almost out of touch with this level, which is experienced only in deep mystical excursions such as meditation. The spiritual triad, like the Divine or supernal one above that has direct connection through Keter with the World of Emanation, has little meaning to those who are unaware of the Worlds hidden beyond the face of the physical world and the images of the ordinary ego mind. For those who wish to experience and explore this inner reality, a glimpse of these upper Worlds is given over and above the moment of religious awe at Creation that every human being has at least once in a lifetime.

The psyche as a whole is as complete an organism as the body. It has present within it many processes parallel to the physical. The ego is the autonomic system of the psyche and the self the central control. The soul is the psyche's metabolism of balance and inner health, and the triad of the spirit is that zone where another World comes into range. Like the body, the psyche runs according to unconscious laws, and a person may be born, live and die without utilizing a fraction of its potential. The Kabbalist endeavours to actualize his full capacity, in order not only to perceive the higher Worlds but to participate in them in a conscious way. However, before the individual can come to this, it first must be realized that such a possibility is there, and that there are others who have the knowledge and experience to train him. Often, all he has to begin with is a few strange moments of vision, one or two books that expound what the ordinary world cannot even recognize, and a deep need to seek and find a key to the Eden from which he dimly remembers his soul came.

Seeking

The Book of Genesis describes how the Worlds of Creation, Formation and Action came into being, and how mankind came to descend into the natural realm; Exodus is concerned with the ascent, back towards the Source. The Sefer Torah (a title which means 'Book of Instruction', and not, as many believe, 'Book of Law') is the teaching embedded in the Old Testament and in the five Books of Moses in particular. This instruction, woven into a framework of ancient cosmic myth, tribal saga and legislation, is directly related to the human situation in that it describes in symbolic form the conditions in which we find ourselves at birth and the method by which we may make our way back to the Promised Land from which we came.

In Judaism there are two lines of biblical knowledge, the written and the oral. The former is incorporated in the biblical canon, and the latter is hinted at in the rabbinical commentaries of the Talmud, which some still call 'oral' although they have been written texts for centuries. The truly oral line is that which is imparted directly from a teacher to a pupil with whom he has an esoteric relationship based on a spiritual level of comprehension. This is the method of Kabbalah, which means 'receiving'. What is imparted in this way has usually been cast in the form of a biblical analogue, and so most Kabbalists working within the orthodox tradition have been deeply versed in the Bible. Thus any chapter, verse or indeed letter may be transformed into a key for comprehending what lies behind a text that is most carefully constructed to hold the secrets of existence.

The account of Jacob's family descending into Egypt is a description of the incarnation of the soul. Mizraim, the Hebrew name for Egypt, means 'confined' and 'limited'. And so it is for the soul, whose natural habitat is the garden of Eden (the World of Yezirah). Here below, in Egypt, the soul is enslaved and after a while forgets the land it came from. Sometimes, however, in spite of the weight of flesh and the preoccupations of work, pain and pleasure, a moment of tranquillity brings to mind that other, freer, place, the dimly recalled homeland. For most people this phenomenon fades in youth, as passion and ambition engage the attention, and the haven we grieved for in childhood is lost beneath the common concern for work or family. Nevertheless, for some this connection is never quite lost, and they seek out the places and the people that help to evoke this faint memory of another World. Most find it spoken of in books; but, alas, the visions of poets and prophets remain only as after-images on a page which gives no map or directions for finding the way back to that far country. Such people, called outsiders by some, are still slaves, like all their fellows bound in the flesh, but they are particularly unhappy ones because they know that they are enslaved and cannot, like their companions, simply lose themselves in the games of everyday life. They want to escape, because they suspect there is more purpose in existence than to feed and propagate like the plants, or to socialize and dominate like the animals.

Often such an outsider runs away, like the young Moses, from his society. Moses' killing of the Egyptian (Exodus 2:11–12) is a symbolic act of severing his connection with the vegetable and animal levels, even though, as an intelligent and privileged man, he held a high position in Egypt. His wanderings in the desert, described in great detail in Jewish folktale, would be familiar to many dropouts in every age. So, too, would his encounter with Jethro, who was to become his father-in-law and his spiritual teacher. In the story in the Talmud, Moses is made to pull from the ground a deep-rooted sapphire rod, engraved with the Names of God, before he can marry Jethro's daughter. This device, familiar in esoteric literature as an initiatory test, is necessary before any further instruction can be given.

The incident of the Burning Bush (Exodus 3) is the culmination, according to rabbinical stories, of several years' training under Jethro. It denotes the state of Grace imparted to a person who has reached a crucial level of inner accomplishment when he can be given responsibility. Moses's initial reluctance to go back to Egypt and fulfil his mission (Exodus 4) is likewise typical of the initial opposition of self will to Divine Will, before the state of submission which says 'Not my will but Thy Will be done.' On accepting his

*I am the man who has girded his loins
And will not pause till his oath is fulfilled,
Whose divided heart wrestles with itself,
Whose soul despises its fleshly home,
Who chose, as a child, the Path of Wisdom.*
Rabbi Solomon ibn Gabirol. Spain, 11th century (from Night-storm, translated by David Goldstein).

destiny, Moses returns to his people to help bring them up out of the house of bondage and into the land flowing with milk and honey, or into the higher Worlds. In personal terms, this means inwardly to educate the undisciplined parts of oneself and outwardly to teach others seeking initiation.

The allegory of Exodus for the Kabbalist has great personal significance because it relates to the conditions of early life and spiritual development. A person is born into and under the laws of a very tough physical existence, where he has to learn the arts and sciences of survival before he is ready to study Kabbalah. This is why one may be accepted by a teacher only upon maturity (which is not always at forty, the age traditionally spoken of: many great Kabbalists died younger). Then one has to undergo a long training, just as Moses tended Jethro's sheep, which may be seen as learning how to command the instincts and impulses of the body and psyche. The Burning Bush episode is the moment when a person makes his own inner connection and must leave his teacher to begin his own work; but this is many years removed from the first stages of spiritual awakening.

While the initial desire to escape from the bondage of Egypt is very strong, the ability to do so may not be there. Many sensitive souls have given up the search for freedom and sunk back into human vegetable and animal realms to become cynical or worse, diabolical, because they do actually know more than those around them. The magician Balaam in the Book of Numbers represents such a person. The seeker will meet these dark but powerful individuals during his search for truth, and for a while he may well be taken in by the knowledge they display to impress. Time or some selfish action will show, however, that such an individual has turned spiritual knowledge into magical power. These encounters are a necessary part of the training designed by Providence, which begins to take an active interest in the genuine seeker.

The phenomenon of Providence becomes increasingly apparent during the seeker's hunt for the door into the upper Worlds, in that certain books turn up at a crucial moment or a meeting occurs with a person who may prove to be a connection with some esoteric tradition. Moses arriving at the well just when Jethro's daughters were being harassed by local shepherds is an example of Providential timing. Such an encounter may lead to an instant connection, but more likely to a series of conversations with an initiate over many years in which the seeker does not realize that he is being checked as a candidate for initiation himself. Such a method gives many traditions, including Kabbalah, the reputation of being secret. One Polish rabbi, for instance, did not even know the profession of his teacher because he had been taught Kabbalah via this technique of discreet instruction. The next step on the path is often to become aware that the person instructing one is not on his own, but part of a link in an ancient chain of teaching. Many academic scholars of Kabbalah find this phenomenon disconcerting, because there is little or no literal evidence of the inner workings and organization of the living tradition; but this is exactly what is meant by an oral line.

Schools of Kabbalah have existed down the centuries, and occasionally they have left accounts of their esoteric meetings and even descriptions of their theories and practices. However, these were usually written down or published long after the esoteric events that brought them into being, because such groups, in contrast to the continuous progress of the more formal side of religion, surface only if that is the need of the epoch. For example, it is known that there was a major Kabbalistic school in the thirteenth century at Gerona in Spain, and at another in the sixteenth century at Safed in Palestine. However, very little of their inner teaching was set down, despite the volume of writing produced in these places. Moreover, not all Kabbalistic schools are necessarily Jewish, or even Bible-orientated. Christian and occult Kabbalah were practised in medieval France, Flanders and Italy, and were not unknown in seventeenth-century Germany and eighteenth-century America. Further, Kabbalah, while remaining a principally Jewish tradition, has affected both Islamic and Christian mysticism and vice versa. Kabbalah has, alas, also been misused both by Jews and Gentiles for magical practices, and this together with its half-understood application by some of the followers of Shabbetai Zvi, a seventeenth-century messianic figure, has brought the name of the Tradition into disrepute. However, so ancient a line of spiritual knowledge can survive any vicissitudes, and not even the onslaught of the age of so-called scientific reason has prevented it from emerging when needed in a contemporary form for the seekers of this generation.

To return to the inner journey out of bondage: when an individual reaches a point of development when he or she knows there is quite definitely more to life than the games people play, and wishes to participate in the work of the higher Worlds, then quite often some remarkable event occurs that changes the course of life. This is symbolized by the crossing of the Red Sea, when an unexpected change, perhaps of job or relationship, occurs in one's life and constitutes a point of no return. After such an event one can no longer merely think or read about spiritual development. There has to be a real commitment. When this is given, then the connection with the spiritual mentor is usually opened up to some group in which the person can actually meet and work with others on the way. Here the story of the Exodus from Egypt becomes a living reality, as one starts on the journey through the desert of the psyche towards the land of the spirit.

Training

As the going out of Egypt involved several stages, so too does the rising out of the normal state of physical and psychological bondage. Usually, during the attempt to take leave of the dominance of the body and ego, a dramatic series of crises or plagues disrupts the life of the person. The typical pattern is of a changing relationship to one's intimates, social status, profession and possessions. On one's own this change cannot be easily sustained, and so the presence of others in a group, symbolized by the Israelites, with a teacher, like Moses, is necessary. Moreover, once the Red Sea has been crossed there is no going back; although some habits, symbolized by the complaining Israelites (Exodus 16:2–3), rebel and yearn to return to the fleshpots of the 'unawakened' condition. In a group the members, under the

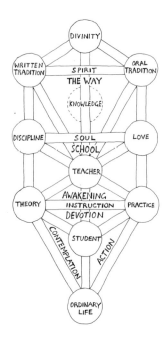

The Way of Kabbalah

*How can you expect me to be perfect
... when I am full of contradictions?
Rabbi Abraham ibn Ezra. Spain, 12th
century.*

guidance of their leader, keep each other from slipping back into slavery. This is done by the Kabbalistic work carried out not only in the group but in everyday life.

The mode of this work, or Avodah in Hebrew, which also means 'service' and 'worship', is based upon the model of the Tree. The first phase is centred around the Sefirah Malkhut, which relates to the practical comprehension of the four elemental states. Here such material problems as getting to a certain place at a certain time are treated as exercises. So, too, are everyday things. As one eighteenth-century Kabbalist remarked, 'I come to observe how my teacher ties up his bootlaces.' This helps one to develop an acute awareness of the elemental world and to recognize how everything physical is in a continuous state of change. This sensitivity is intensified until it is realized that indeed all four Worlds are present within one's own body and within the physical Universe.

The next step, with the help of the others and the teacher, is to identify the nature of the Yesodic ego. This is done by different members of the group giving examples of their own thinking, feeling and acting processes as coloured by their particular education, bias and blind spots. The basis for this threefold view is in the three small triads that feed the Yesod of the ego and compose the great triad of the vegetable or routine processes of the psyche. In this way the student becomes familiar with the Tree at work within himself as he sees the active side of the psyche stimulate action and feeling and the passive side restrain feeling and lead to reflective thought. In Kabbalah the method is called the study of action, devotion and contemplation. In this the student carries out various exercises such as performing a sacred act – perhaps that of lighting a candle before reciting a prayer in the heart – or considering a Kabbalistic idea for a week, at the end of which he reports to the group for comment and comparison. In this way he becomes acquainted with his own particular ego type and its imbalances, so that he perceives that he is primarily a thinker, feeler or doer and can work on the other two ego-centred triads in order to correct any deficiency.

The next stage is to examine the qualities of the two Sefirot of bio-psychological function, Hod and Nezah. These two are particularly difficult to define because of their wide variety of activity. In the organization of a Kabbalistic group they relate to theory and practice. Theory is set upon the passive column of Form at Hod, because it is concerned with the learning, monitoring and feedback processes. This expresses itself in the study of texts and Kabbalistic diagrams, as well as in the examination of words and numbers. It might equally be the detailed analysis of a parable, or the collection of data on a recurring principle to see how it is rooted in a particular Sefirah. The energy of Nezah, being active as against reflective, is concerned with practice; this can be manifested in several ways. A special ritual might be designed in the group to be enacted to evoke a Sefirotic triad; or there might be a practical exercise of Kabbalistic principles at work in life, such as applying the metaphysics of the Tree to medical or business problems. Likewise, a building or ritual object based upon Kabbalistic theory can be constructed with particular attention given during the work to prayer or a certain idea such as the unity of earth and heaven.

The teacher (or Maggid) stands at the Tiferet or watcher position, in relation to the student at the group collective and personal Yesod. He acts as the guiding self to the student's as yet undisciplined ego, just as Moses did to the slave-minded Israelites. From this Seat of Solomon directions are given, not just by the Maggid himself but by that which passes through him from above through the paths coming from the other Sefirot of the group Tree. In this way the Maggid's personal imbalances are checked and a flow descends from the higher Worlds, for the most part unimpaired, to the students below. In this way the chain of teaching takes on a totally different dimension and scale. Some great Kabbalists have said they have been taught by Elijah who is the link between Heaven and Earth. On the Tree of instruction this is where the Malkhut of the World of the spirit (Beriah) meets the Tiferet of the psyche (Yezirah) and the Keter of the body (Asiyyah). Thus Kabbalah is imparted and received all down the line of Worlds from Metatron, the highest initiate, to the most modest student, provided he is receptive.

When the student reaches the level of Tiferet in himself – that is, when he has developed enough will to cross the triad of awakening whenever he wishes – he becomes his own tutor. This is because he comes into contact with the soul triad (Hesed, Gevurah and Tiferet) which brings the discipline of Justice and the tolerance of Mercy into play. This emotional triad, pivoted upon the self, works at refining a now self conscious soul, sometimes by a touch of Severity from the left and sometimes by a touch of Mercy from the right, which, perceived from the self, brings into balance some discrepancy of emotional expansion or contraction. This work, carried out with and for others in the group, continues over many years : Kabbalah is an undramatic tradition that requires great patience and stability. One of the reasons for this tempo is that everyone has to mature his potential gradually and thoroughly at his natural pace. In this way his life's work unfolds at the right moment in his own and the cosmos's time. This timing relates to the destiny of individuals and schools which meet the needs of the seen and unseen Worlds according to the configuration of a particular point in history.

In group terms, the great upper triad of the spirit is concerned with such cosmic matters as generating new religious or social epochs (as against the more individual affairs of the lower part of the Tree). Here Binah and Hokhmah, the Sefirot of tradition and revelation, with the non-Sefirah of Knowledge, Daat, supply to any who can reach this level a celestial or panhistoric view of events. This is seen in the biblical prophecies, and also in the Kabbalistic schemes of the Universe that have been handed down in manuscript or by word of mouth over the generations. Any student of Kabbalah has access to these levels, but not necessarily just through being a member of a particular group or sect or by having a whole library of Kabbalistic books. A deep inner connection has to be developed so that there is a personal contact with what has been called the Academy on High. Other traditions have called this level of reality the Isle of Saints, the Inner Circle of Mankind, or the Great Brotherhood of Initiates. It has no location in this world; its place is in the upper part of Yezirah (the psyche) and the lower part of Beriah (the spirit). It is outside ordinary time and space.

The topmost triad of the group Tree is the direct contact with the Divine.

Corresponding to the levels within the individual as well as the group, this is the place where it is possible to come into the presence of the Shekhinah or the place of the Lord. Some people experience this spontaneously in an act of Grace as a state of profound awe in which they are filled and surrounded by golden light and a sense of unity and peace. The Kabbalist seeks this act of Yehud or Unity consciously, with others or alone, under the wings of the tradition where Knowledge allows and aids the knower and known to be one.

Kabbalistic groups generally work inside a disciplined setting. Operating within the oral tradition, they may be found all over the world, and not always inside Jewish orthodoxy. To find them is not easy, and certainly to be invited to enter a group is even more difficult, because only people who want to develop all the levels of their nature can work in Kabbalah. Many who are frightened or fascinated by Kabbalah know of it only via a superstitious and often ill-informed image, and sometimes even the learned on the subject are more ignorant of its true nature than those who have had a passing contact with it. Kabbalah only opens its door to those who are prepared to receive. A fable adapted from the Kabbalistic classic, the Zohar, illustrates the point.

A certain young man once saw the figure of a veiled girl at the window of a palace. At first only curious, he went each day to catch a glimpse of her. After a while, she would look in his direction as if expecting him. Slowly he became involved in what appeared to be a relationship if only at a distance. In the course of time the girl lowered her veil to reveal something of her face. This so increased his interest that he spent many hours at the palace hoping to see the fullness of her beauty. Gradually he fell deeply in love with her and spent most of his day at her window. Over time she became more open with him and they conversed, she telling of the secrets of the palace and the nature of her father the King. Eventually he could bear it no longer and wished only to be joined with her in marriage so that he might experience all she spoke of. The man in this allegory is the soul, the princess the spirit, the palace existence, and the King the King of Kings.

He who shall know the mystery of the Gates of Understanding in the Kabbalah shall know also the Mystery of the Great Jubilee [the completion of the spiritual cycle].
Pico della Mirandola, Christian Kabbalist. Italy, 15th century.

Work of Unification

After the initial training in theory and practice comes the pursuit of unification and perfection, that is the bringing together of the body and psyche and the harmonizing of their component parts into an accord with the higher Worlds. For most Kabbalists the various stages of unification are obtained by the merit of diligent work, although, as one rises up through the seven levels of the psyche, Grace sometimes descends to meet one and grant profound Yeziratic or psychological insights and Beriatic or spiritual experiences. These can never be explained in ordinary terms, although in Kabbalistic writings down the ages traces have been left that describe a pattern of phenomena recognized in other esoteric traditions.

The techniques used by Kabbalists are many and varied, but they all generally fit into the three definitions of action, devotion and contemplation, following the laws of the three ego triads. *Actions* such as the

One may learn even from a thief. He is
ever watchful, takes every opportunity
and does not despise the least gain. A
Kabbalist should use the same criteria
for inner development.
Hasidic Rabbi. Poland, 18th century.

performance of the daily physical routine become transformed into testimonies of sacred ritual. These may lie in such obvious ceremonies as the binding of the *tefilin*, prayer boxes, on to the arm and head of the orthodox Jew; but they may also be a keen attention to all ordinary activities, that they may be dedicated to God. As one Russian Kabbalist said, 'If one can think of business during prayer, then one can pray while doing business.' *Devotional* exercises based both upon love and fear of God may be carried out at any moment; the Kabbalist observes the Glory of the Divine present in the world about him, and so he continually gives thanks for rain, food, family and even the crises that periodically disrupt the rhythm of life because they are sent by Providence to teach this or that lesson. Nothing is seen as insignificant, everything is a gift of God to be appreciated. Even the threat of or contact with evil is perceived as a blessing, an act of love in disguise. The continuous act of *contemplation* is carried out by all Kabbalists, for Kabbalah is principally a Way of Knowledge. This is to say that, while many believers may find that to love or fear God, or to carry out the Commandments, is sufficient, the Kabbalist wishes to know God, and to this end studies both the microcosm of himself and the macrocosm of the universe in order to become familiar with God's ways. Such an intellectual contemplative approach is considerably aided by an ever-deepening knowledge of the Sefirotic Tree, which continually reveals in its living structure facet after facet and depth upon depth of the Creator's Will to behold Divinity in everything.

During all this long labour many transformations occur, both within and without. At first everything is exciting, with the discovery that there is an answer to every question; often the individual's whole life style is radically altered. Then there follows a dull period in which little seems to happen except in gradual shifts that seem insignificant by contrast with the first dramatic period. This quiet phase, however, is a preparation, a prelude to inner events that slowly emerge from the World of the spirit, through the deep layers of the psyche and into ordinary consciousness. Such a shift may take the form of a gradual reorientation to one's Kabbalistic circle or an alteration in one's whole view of the four Worlds. A doctor, for example, may come to see his professional role Kabbalistically as part of a great impulse to bring conventional medicine into contact with inner healing, as he perceives he is being inwardly trained for work that is in no direct way related to his original ambition of being a specialist. A man or woman might begin to realize the power to raise the ethical level in business by his or her mere presence, or acquire the ability to see or hear over great distances, or even directly into the upper Worlds, for the benefit of others without such sight. These are gifts that come naturally with inner evolution, without the artificial aids of magical or occult techniques. As one of the greatest Kabbalists said, 'Seek ye first the Kingdom of Heaven [that is the Malkhut of Beriah] and all else will be added unto you.'

Accounts of interior visions have come down to us in fragments. Some of these documents also describe the physical and psychological conditions needed before such events can occur. Very often fasting or intense exertion is used as a preparation, as is solitude or sexual abstinence. These techniques vary according to epoch and school, but all seek to obtain the same state of being in balance and lucidity. One set of instructions recommended for example satisfying the body so that it should not intrude, while another directive suggested the continuous and rapid writing of random Hebrew letters so as to overload and confuse the ordinary Yesodic mind; yet another perceived the act of sexual love as a method of entering the upper Worlds. Kabbalah is wide enough to accommodate anything from ecstatic dancing to absolute stillness and inner silence.

In ancient times the process of going deep into oneself during ritual, meditation or contemplation was called 'going down in the Chariot'. This action simultaneously precipitated the rising up out of the physical world and through what were called the seven lower or lesser Halls of the psyche (see p. 91). These steps comprised an awareness of the body, the Yeziratic Malkhut, the ordinary ego state at Yesod, the Hod, Nezah, Tiferet condition of awakening, the consciousness of the soul triad, then the spiritual and Divine triads at the Crown of the Yeziratic Tree. This prepared the way into the seven Greater Halls of the Beriatic World. In this ordered and disciplined progression Kabbalists enter and experience the World of Creation while still in the flesh and see the panorama of the Heavens and their inhabitants. Such an inner journey, however, is fraught with hazard for the immature, the unbalanced and the wrongly motivated. An ancient account of four rabbis who entered the World of pure spirit is often given as a warning against unprepared excursion into the realm of Heaven. The first died, the second went mad, and the third became a disbeliever. Only the fourth, Rabbi Akiba, came back safely to tell of what he saw. What follows is a precis of his experience.

In the first Hall, which corresponds to the Kingdom of Creation or the spiritual aspect of the Self, Akiba says that he was in a state of Hasid devotion. Here, where what is called the Vilon, the Veil of Heaven, is rolled away, he entered the World of pure spirit. From this place where angels and humans may converse he rose in Tahor, a state of purity, to the second Heavenly Hall, called Rakiyah or the Firmament, where the great archangel Gabriel is said to reside. Here in the Yesod of Beriah, the Foundation of Creation, is the level where the signs of Heaven are revealed to the prophets. It is also the place of the Holy Spirit in man and corresponds to Daat, the non-Sefirah of Knowledge in his psyche. The third level is called Shehakim, the Skies, and here in a condition of Yashar, sincerity, Akiba was in the third Heaven, where the millstones of the Universe slowly turn to grind out Time. He then rose to the fourth Heaven, where he came into direct contact with the Divine in a situation of Tamim or wholeness: this is the place where the three upper Worlds meet, as the Tiferet of Beriah and the Malkhut of Azilut, the Kingdom of the Divine, touch the Keter of Yezirah, the Crown of the psyche. At this level, occupied by the great archangel Michael, is the Heavenly Jerusalem and its Temple. Passing beyond the normal limits of the human psyche, because he had developed a stable spiritual vehicle, Akiba entered the fifth Heaven, called Maon, or Dwelling, where he encountered the great archangelic guardians Samael and Zadkiel, in front of whom he had to speak the Kedushah prayer of sanctification Holy! Holy! Holy! to demonstrate his holiness before he could pass on to the sixth Heaven of Makom or the Omnipresent, where he came into the company

And I went in till I drew nigh to a wall which was built of crystals and surrounded by tongues of fire: and it began to affright me. And I went into the tongues of fire and drew nigh to a large house which was built of crystals: and the walls of the house were like a tesselated flow of crystal, and its groundwork was of crystal. Its ceiling was like the path of the stars and the lightning, and between them were fiery cherubim and their heaven was [clear as] water.
Ethiopic Book of Enoch 1. Palestine, 2nd century BCE (translated by R. H. Charles).

of the highest created beings before the celestial Throne. Here he sang with the heavenly choir the praises of God, into Whose Presence he came when he ascended into the seventh Heaven, the Great Hall of the Arabot. Here he stood 'erect, holding his balance with all his might', as he trembled before his Creator.

Akiba then descended safely out of the Presence of the Divine, down through the seven states of the spirit into the seven lesser Halls or levels of the psyche, and back into the body, because he was well grounded in ordinary life. In Kabbalah this stability is an absolute prerequisite because any major flaw or imbalance in body or psyche is magnified during such an experience. Thus the Kabbalist does not withdraw from the lower Worlds and seek special conditions or isolation in which to develop, but uses the daily situation and ordinary events about him both as a working method and as an anchor for the moments when he enters the highly charged and rarified levels of the upper Worlds. There is, moreover, another reason why the Kabbalist does not retire or seek to escape from the lower Worlds; and this is a fundamental difference between Kabbalah and certain other spiritual traditions. Kabbalah does not regard matter as evil, nor the natural World as undesirable or inhibiting to the soul or spirit. It is part of one whole. How could it be otherwise? Existence emanates from God, and therefore while there are degrees of increasing separation, not a fraction of existence exists for a second without Divine Will: not even evil, which has its own cosmic task to perform.

Everything in the universe is of a piece, like a seamless garment that God has wrapped about Divinity. Kabbalah recognizes, however, because there are four Worlds, each with a complex of levels and functions, that there can be apparently different realities. Thus the Tachutonim, those creatures that dwell below in the natural kingdom, cannot perceive the Elyonim, or those who dwell above. Only Man has the capability of perceiving both the superior and inferior Worlds. To acquire such an inner and outer faculty of sight is one of the aims of Kabbalah, for its theory and practice enable individuals to expand their consciousness down and up, and if necessary bridge the gap between the Worlds so as to bring about an increased flow of Divine and celestial influx to bear where evolution is delayed, where disorder is prevalent, or where harmony needs to be encouraged, or consciousness of the Presence of the Divine to be made manifest in the midst of humanity.

Such operations are the ultimate work of Kabbalah. While one may experience as an individual the higher landscapes of Creation, glimpse the government of Heaven and even perceive angelic beings about their business, this may remain no more than a personal spiritual trip, like those apparently described in some of the early mystical accounts. This is a pitfall spoken of in many spiritual traditions, as are the dangers of acquiring supernatural powers through ego-motivated concentration on particular psychic faculties. The Work of Unification is not concerned only with individual development, but with helping to bring about the unity of the Worlds that are still in the travail of Creation. As the personal levels of body, psyche, spirit and Divine spark are brought into harmony, so the Kabbalist seeks to be used in assisting existence towards his and its own destiny. This

An individual should hold an awareness of God and His love all the time. He should not separate his consciousness from the Divine while he journeys on the way, nor when he lies down nor when he rises up. Rabbi Nahmanides. Spain, 13th century.

is to become an individual mirror within the cosmic mirror in which the little Adam of a man may gaze into the ever-increasing depths of the image of the Great Adam of the universe and so perceive the reflection of the Divine. In this way each Kabbalist, in company with every other person on the path of spiritual tradition, aids God to behold God long before the majority of humanity begins to become aware of the purpose of life beyond ordinary living. This participation in the Divine plan is called the Work of Creation.

Work of Creation

As Creation emerged out of the World of the Sefirot to begin the cosmic Week of Days, so Time was called forth out of Eternity. The motion of Creation, Formation and Action will be continuous until the End of Days when the mission of existence is accomplished. At this point in the process of outflowing and return we are, according to Kabbalistic tradition, about mid-way, as the extreme of matter has been reached and the awakening consciousness of evolution begins to raise the level of the universe out of the mineral, vegetable and animal stages into the incarnate human stage. Thus, taking our own immediate area of the universe, the Milky Way has progressed enough to refine into a distinct spiral formation with a structure composed of atom-based stars which in turn have evolved molecular-based planets; and on the surface of one there exists cell-based organic life. This order of the evolutionary chain may well be common to other galaxies and solar systems and include minerals, plants, animals and humanoids which would be not entirely unfamiliar to mankind: this notion is based upon the principle that all organisms are based on the same Sefirotic model, which generates creatures that possess will, intellect, emotion and capability of action.

The planet Earth, after entering fiery, gaseous, liquid and solid phases, has acquired what appears to be a relative stability. In the long term, this is illusory; cosmic rhythms when perceived on their own time scale are anything but static or undramatic. For example, it is only in the last few million years that conditions have been suitable for life, and of this period only a fraction has produced mankind. On this scale of time human history reveals a drama of rapidly unfolding events, as periods of crisis and quiet unfold with episodes within rhythms as one part of mankind emerges to dominate the scene, as in the Mediterranean world the Greeks gave way to Rome, which was then superseded by the Arabs. All these flowerings and witherings correspond to planetary and stellar fluctuations, and are the human response to the cosmic tension between order and chaos which is seen in the personal sphere as the conflict between good and evil.

According to some Kabbalists, the moment Creation separated from the World of Emanation there emerged the principle of evil. Now evil is not always what it appears to be. There are different kinds of evil. The highest form is self will; this is embodied in the archangel Lucifer, who rebelled against God. He manifests all the way down through the Worlds as the principle that always knows better, and he is found in the proud and arrogant on every level. Then there is the role of the Tempter, who has one of

When the Holy One who created the Universe wished to reveal its hidden aspect, the light within darkness, He showed how things were inter-mingled. Thus out of darkness comes light and from the concealed comes the revealed. In the same manner does good emerge from evil and Mercy from Justice, since they too are intertwined.
Zohar. Spain, 13th century.

the dirty jobs in existence. This requires great skill, and it is here that Lucifer, who performs this task, uses his excessive cleverness. The snake in Genesis is the same manifestation, as is Satan in Job. These types of evil belong to the central Pillar of the Tree and are concerned with consciousness. However, there are also evil elements associated with the side Pillars of function. These are evils generated by the excessive contraction of too much Form or Severity, or by the excessive expansion of too much Force or Mercy. These evils are embodied in the demonic remnants of the previous Worlds that existed before this universe. As such, they carry out the work of testing and tempering the processes and products of Creation. For example, we see them in the tensions set up by extremes of wealth or privation in human society. The last and lowest kind of evil is not really evil at all; its results appear harmful or unpleasant, but are not. Such natural processes as excretion, death and dissolution are the refuse phases of the Creative, Formative and Active cycles, and without them the universe would be cluttered up.

In the Divine plan mankind has a crucial role to play. According to tradition, each individual is sent down to accomplish a task that is related to a special aspect of the whole scheme. Clearly this is not possible in one lifetime, and so Kabbalah subscribes to the idea of reincarnation, called Gilgulim or the Turnings in Hebrew. Our free will, leading to wilful, will-less or willing actions, generates what in India is called Karma, and in Kabbalah reward and punishment ('unto the third and fourth generation'). When this multi-dimensional picture of human destiny is perceived, we see that an individual is not only a cell of Adam Kadmon, with certain gifts and properties, but an entity that is periodically born into a physical body in order to accomplish its task. Thus birth and rebirth is no random event but a carefully organized operation under what is called the Supervision of Heaven which, as the general cosmic agency of Divine Will, has command of all in the lower Worlds. Such ancient names for Kabbalists as 'Those Who Know' and 'The Reapers of the Field' refer to this dimension and explain why many of them have deep affection for or knowledge of other periods and countries. They were there, carrying out the Work of Creation.

The Work of Creation for mankind is conscious participation in the realization of the Divine intention. In this the Kabbalist not only makes himself more and more aware of the events in the greater and unseen Worlds above but actually helps to bring in the influxes descending from the upper into the lower Worlds. He does this by being skilful in practical life, psychologically sound and spiritually clear. This makes him a good instrument to carry out any task Providence may assign him. It means that he not only unconsciously performs according to his fate, as many do, but acts from knowledge, so that he can adjust and adapt an event or action in order to fill it with greater light, purity, balance and efficiency: to endow it, in other words, with the qualities of all four Worlds. An example of this was the great eighteenth-century teacher and Kabbalist Baal Shem Tov, who brought about a profound spiritual revival in a desolated Jewish community in eastern Europe. This could only be done while he was in the flesh.

The idea of the presence of such developed people upon the earth, who are here by choice, is common to all spiritual traditions. In Kabbalah the

Every soul is subject to the trial of Transmigration . . . An individual does not know that he is called for assessment before entering this World as well as after leaving it. He does not know how many transformations and esoteric trials he has to pass through . . . and that souls revolve like a stone shot from a sling.
Zohar. Spain, 13th century.

29

fable of the Lamed Vav, the thirty-six just men, hints at the presence of a brotherhood, scattered round the globe, of wise beings who watch over the spiritual life of mankind. At this level they may well be Hindus sitting in Himalayan caves, Muslims working silver in Damascus, Christians practising medicine in London or Jews teaching economics in Russia. No one but they, we are told, knows who the thirty-six are, because to the world they appear quite naturally within their everyday context. Tradition goes further and hints at a whole hierarchy of spiritually evolved people, with each level concerned with a different stage of mankind's progress. Some of these individuals may be well known to the public, others hidden, as is the one who is called in Islam 'the Axis of the Age'. In Kabbalah this most perfected of incarnate humans is the representative of the Messiah, who acts as the connection between all the Worlds. In this one man all the levels possible at this point in incarnate evolution have been unified, and he acts as the spearhead for mankind. Such a person is said to be present in every generation, so that the usual conception of the Messiah as having been, or being yet to come, takes on the dimension of the Divine, which is 'I Was, I Am, and I Will Be'. To Kabbalists it could be no other way, except that the Messiah will, at the approach of the End of Days, become known openly to all mankind when the Work of Creation approaches its final perfection.

Completion

The Work of Creation is slowly refining the mirror of existence into a higher and more subtle state in order to reflect in the evolving consciousness of Adam a clearer and more lucid image of God. Thus, as the macrocosm develops, so mankind, as it spreads throughout all the Worlds, looks both outward and inward, so creating an increasing unity above and below. This is observable in the evidence of the earth, which has continually refined the fabric of its elements and the quality of life upon its surface. In the short time human beings have been involved in the planet's affairs we have moved from tribes of nomadic hunters into agricultural peoples from which nations, then empires, and then civilizations have evolved. It is true that many of these larger units of humanity have exhibited the more savage traits of mankind, but it can also be observed that tribal custom has given way to the rule of law in varying degrees of Wisdom, Understanding, Truth, Justice and Mercy. This has come about by the presence of wise and enlightened people behind every step in civilization who have shown, by example, the higher way to think, feel and act. Such work is a quiet pressure over thousands of years, sustained by countless known and unknown men and women edging the human race towards perfection, and periodically stimulated by such messianic teachers as Buddha, Moses, Jesus and Muhammad.

It can be said that mankind has emerged from its vegetable period of mere survival, and is now in its animal stage, where nations like animals are still striving for dominance. However, the next step up through the Worlds appears to be emerging, in that there is not only a physical global awareness through mass communications, but an increasing psychological sensitivity to the rights of men and women. Moreover, in some parts of the world there has been in recent years a deepening interest in spiritual matters; and so the slow unification of the three lower Worlds of mankind can be detected at an economic or vegetable level, a political or animal level, a psychological or soul level and an ecumenical or spiritual level.

According to the laws embodied in all the Worlds, there are times when the balance is momentarily out to one side, and so there are some epochs of tremendous activity and others in which little happens, just as in a man's life. In these periods things can go wrong, because the demonic forces both within and without seek to impose their will. In such periods some people will work to hold the balance while others will, out of perversity or self-interest, try to aid the forces that disrupt or restrain the new phase that is coming into being. This gives many social and political issues a cosmic or spiritual dimension. The wars of decolonization in Africa illustrate this point. However, we are told, towards the End of Days, when the great cycles of the cosmic Shemittot are drawing to their close, a completely new dimension will arise that only apocalyptic allegory can describe because it involves the upper Worlds more and more directly. The hallmark of this period is said to be the final confrontation between Good and Evil, that is the polarization between those who affirm the aim of Existence and those who seek their own purpose. The former will be represented symbolically and literally by the Messiah who, it is said, will be the last spirit to be incarnated upon this earth and the latter by the anti-Messiah or the most egotistical of beings. After a conflict in which even the skies and nature will express the war in all the Worlds, with strange terrestrial and celestial phenomena, there will, in the defeat of Evil, be total peace and world order reigned over by the Messiah. This period, however, in which Time we are told gradually slows down, is but a prelude to allow everyone to prepare for the Last Judgment at the End of Days.

According to Kabbalah, on this final Day of the cosmic cycle every creature from above and below is brought up before the Throne of Heaven and assessed as regards its performance through the whole of Time. Some are exalted to the heights and others thrown down into the depths as the last hours of Creation draw the separated Worlds closer together in unification. As each creature gazes at the Divine Presence upon the Throne, so it realizes that it is but a facet of a whole. Finally as the last fully realized spirit of mankind blends into Adam Kadmon, so this great image of God looks into the Mirror of Existence to see in the total experience of humanity the reflection of its own Divinity. At that moment perfection is reached in the Union with the Holy Name of I AM THAT I AM when God beholds God. In the radiance of this completion, image merges with reality to dissolve into AYIN SOF and to vanish into AYIN again: Alone, God is God.

Holy, Holy, Holy art Thou, King of the Universe,
Thy Glory fills all the Worlds.

And the Ancient of Days did sit, whose garment was white as snow, and the hair of His Head like pure wool: His Throne was like the fiery flame, and His wheels as burning fire. A fiery stream issued and came forth from before Him: thousand thousands ministered unto Him, and ten thousand times ten thousand stood before Him: the Judgment was set, and the books were opened.
Daniel 7:9–10.

According to tradition, Melchizedek, the King of Righteousness and of Salem, and priest of the Most High God, initiated Abraham into the knowledge of the esoteric Teaching which concerns man, the universe and God. Melchizedek – born, it is said, without father or mother, having neither beginning nor end of life – is traditionally called a son of God abiding for ever. He is seen as the same individual as Enoch, the first initiate, and Elijah, the instructor of the mystics down the ages. Out of this encounter between a celestial and a terrestrial man came the spiritual line known later as Kabbalah. (Melchizedek and Abraham, gold and enamel altar plaque by Nicholas de Verdun at Klosterneuburg, Austria, 12th c.)

VICTOR · ABRAM · REGV̄ · DECIMAVIT · SINGVLA · RERV̄

ABRAHAM MELCHISEĐ

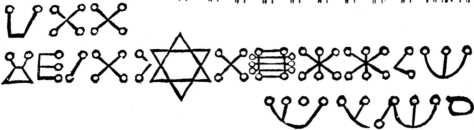

קמ"ט   אחרת לחן ולחסד כתוב על קלף צבי כשר בשמך רחנינה וח סד יהוה   בעולם יהי חסדך יהוה על
סב"ם לכשם שהיה הצדיק שנאמר ויהי ה' את יוסף   ויט אליו חסד ויתן את חנו בעיני כל רואיו
בשם מיכא"ל גבריא"ל רפא"ל אוריא"ל כנשיא"ל יה יה יה יה· יה יה יה· יה אהיה אהה אדה
אדה אהה יהו· יהו· ירו· יהו· יהו· יהו· יהו· יהו· יהו· יהו· יה

קמ"ט   אחרת שלא ישלוט באדם שים כלי זין כתוב בקלף של צבי כשר ותלי בצוארך שמות הקדושים האלו ·
עתריאל וריאל חוריאל המדריאל שובריאל שובראל עורריאל שורריאל
מיכאל גבריאל הגריאל הגדה אל שובריאל צבחר אתניק צורטק אנקתם פסתם
פספסים דיונסים ליש ועת כקו יתי יהוה אבן קרע שטן נגד יכש בטר צתג חקב
טנע יגל פזק ישקרצית קבצקאל אהמנוניאל ומסתיה הירשתיאל עאנה פיה אלעה
אבג יתין אלעה עה עה
עזור לפלוני בן פלוני

It is said that God first taught the secrets of existence to the highest archangels, who formed an inner council at the celestial Court of the Almighty. In this Christian version of the Teaching (in Jewish art there can be no natural representation of God) the Creator prescribes the laws that will govern Creation. These are based, according to the Kabbalah, on the ten Sefirot, Divine Attributes or Manifestations of the Absolute, willed into existence in order that God might behold God. (God the Architect of Creation, from ms., Holkham Bible, England, 14th c.)

It is said that God took compassion on Adam after he had been banished from Eden, and so sent the archangel Raziel, whose name means 'Secrets of God', to give him a book so that man might not only regain entry to the Garden of Paradise but remember that he was, as the image of God, the looker into the mirror of existence wherein he would perceive the Divine Face. This book has been handed down, although degenerate written versions have obscured its content. An oral version still exists in Kabbalah. (Angelic writing, from Book of Raziel, Netherlands, 17th c.)

The first obvious teaching diagram of the Jewish esoteric tradition is the Menorah, the candlestick specified by God to Moses on Mount Sinai (Exodus 25). Made of one piece of pure gold, to represent the unchanging and unified Divine World of Emanation, it is composed of a central axis of Grace, right and left arms of Mercy and Severity, ten plus one Sefirotic positions, and twenty-two decorations. This ritual object is the exoteric form of an esoteric scheme of existence, and is there to be contemplated as well as utilized in worship. (Menorah from Bible in Sefardi hand, 13th c.; diagram showing the Sefirot set out on the Menorah.)

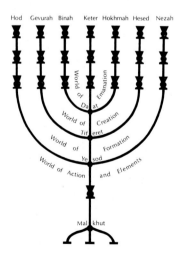

In the Second Temple period of Jewish history (6th century BCE–1st century CE), what is now known as Kabbalah was called the Work of the Chariot. The name comes from the prophetic vision of Ezekiel, whose writings form the basis of much Jewish mystical experience and thought. Chapter 1 of Ezekiel expresses, in the metaphysical language of the time, the hierarchy of Worlds (see pp. 11, 41): the World of Action, on earth; the World of the Chariot, or Formation; the World of the Throne, or Creation; and the Divine World of Emanation, shown as Adam, the likeness of the Glory of God. Such glimpses of the upper Worlds were sought through the so-called Work of the Chariot, despite the dangers involved for the impure, the unbalanced and the untrained. (Ezekiel's vision, from Bear Bible, England, 17th c.)

Kabbalists have made many attempts to formulate the process by which existence came into manifestation. All fail, because it is impossible to encapsulate the Divine in metaphysics. However, mystics have never ceased to attempt such schemes, or to find them useful. In the version shown here the AYIN and AYIN SOF of Absolute Nothing and All contract to leave a void in which the Divine Will manifests ten Divine Attributes. Will is visualized as a beam of light travelling inward from the periphery of Eternal Light (AYIN SOF OR) to call forth, create, form and make the initial manifestation of the Divine, which is Azilut, the World of Emanation. (Zimzum or Contraction: the first manifestation. There is a key to this diagram on p. 6.)

The Shem ha-Meforash, the special Name of God that was given to Moses, can be seen, in a vertical arrangement, as the likeness of Adam Kadmon, the Primordial Man. The Hebrew letters Yod, He, Vav, He are perceived as representing not only the Divine Will, Intellect, Emotion and Action but the four levels of Emanation, Creation, Formation and Making, set out in three Pillars of Will, Mercy and Severity. This figure of the Kavod or Divine Glory, composed of black and white fire, is spoken of in Ezekiel as 'the appearance of a man'. (The Divine Name as Adam Kadmon.)

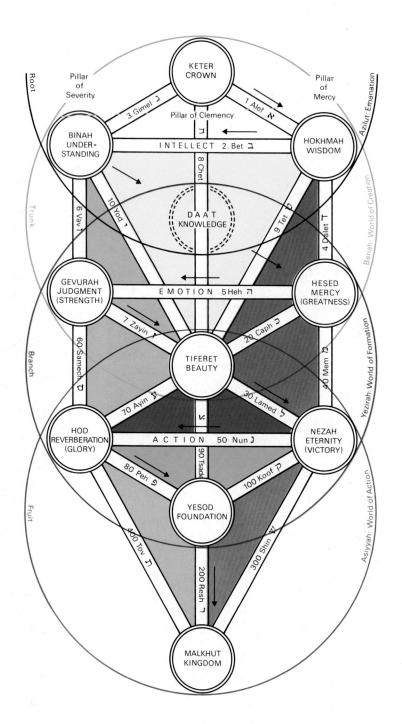

The diagram of the Sefirot or Divine Attributes was not published in full until the Middle Ages. There have been many variations (see, for instance, pp. 72–73); but this is the version used by many Kabbalists today. Its structure contains all the laws that govern existence, because it reveals a universal process of balanced interaction between upper and lower, active (right) and passive (left) principles. The Divine influx can be traced in detail along the paths between the Sefirot (designated by the twenty-two Hebrew letters) and through the triads or three-cornered relationships that link them. The colours here distinguish between functional or side triads (red active and blue passive) and the central triads which denote levels of consciousness and will (green, purple, yellow).

The four large circles show the levels within a single Tree which correspond to the four Worlds (see right-hand page) of Will, Intellect, Emotion and Action. Complex to the highest degree, the Sefirotic Tree is nevertheless an image of Divine Unity. (The Tree of Life, its structure and dynamics. See pp. 6–8, 50–51.)

The extended Tree, which shows the interlocking of the four Worlds, also has many versions. Its colours, as specified in Exodus 26, are white (radiance) for Azilut; blue (heaven) for Beriah; red (blood and earth) for Asiyyah; and purple (union of heaven and earth) for Yezirah, which is a bridge between the upper and lower Worlds. In the scheme shown here, each World or level, with its own sub-Tree, emerges out of the centre of the one above, so that there is an interpenetration of Emanation, Creation, Formation and Action. Thus man, who has within him the four corresponding levels of Divinity, spirit, psyche and body, can perceive all the Worlds in his inner and outer return to the Source. In a gradual process of realization, the fallen Adam becomes increasingly aware of the Divine Presence at every level, and the microcosm beholds in the macrocosm the Image of God. (Jacob's Ladder, the hierarchy of the four Worlds. See p. 90.)

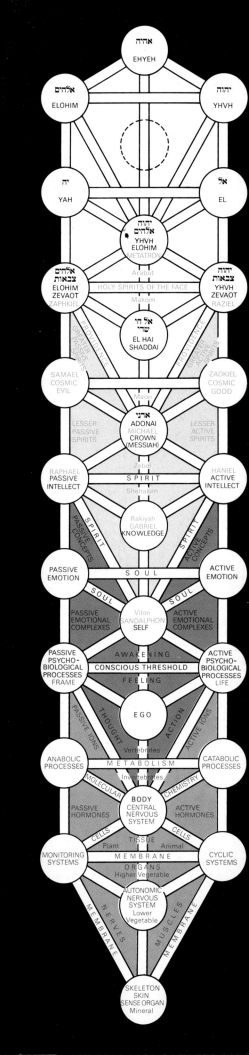

Beriah or Creation is the World in which the Will of God, emanating from the unchanging realm of eternity (the World of Azilut), creates space and time. Genesis 1 describes the opening phases of a cosmic drama whose actors inhabit a World of pure spirit governed by its own cycle of days and seasons. A spiritual Adam, the last of these beings to be created, is the most perfect of them all, with the added gift of free will. This sets the scene for the unfolding of the destiny of mankind. (The Creation of Light, mezzotint by John Martin, England, 19th c.)

If the World of Creation is Heaven, then that of Formation is Eden. Here, things called forth and created as spirit are clothed in qualities and characteristics, like an idea taking shape. In this realm, everything flows through endless metamorphoses, as Creation moves from the beginning to the end of time. Here the Adam of Creation is formed into two sexes, representing the left and right Pillars, while the Tree of knowledge or Creation rises in the midst of the Garden. Above is the Tree of Life, the Divine World of Emanation; below the serpent of wilfulness tests the spirit and the soul. (The Temptation of Adam and Eve, woodcut, France, c. 1500.)

The World of Asiyyah, or Action and Elements, is the last of the four levels to come into manifestation. This is the physical World in which the activities of the upper Worlds work themselves out in practice. The presence of all four Worlds at this physical level is sometimes symbolized through the four traditional elements: fire or light representing Emanation; air representing the spiritual and cosmic processes of Creation; water representing the flux of Formation; and earth as the solid ground of existence. In this view the lowest level of manifestation – furthest removed from pure Divinity and subject to the greatest number of laws – is nevertheless the repository of all that has gone before. Thus, while everything perceived by the senses may be physical, to the Kabbalist all phenomena are the effects of causes that have come down through all the levels of existence. A landscape at sunset, with its elements of solid matter, shifting symbolic forms, atmosphere and light, thus takes on physical, psychological, spiritual and Divine dimensions. (Jerusalem.)

With the World of Creation came the first separation from the Divine. Here, at one remove from direct contact with Divinity, evil came into being. This is traditionally figured in the archangel Lucifer's revolt against the Divine ordinance that he should submit himself to Adam. For this rebellion Lucifer was cast out to take on the task of the tempter. He works with the demonic forces of disintegration to test the integrity of Creation, and especially that of man, the only creature to possess free will. The archangel Michael (see p. 74) was ordained to be the adversary of evil in heaven, while man is responsible for order upon earth. (The conflict between good and evil, order and chaos, detail of The Last Judgment, triptych by Hieronymus Bosch, Netherlands, c. 1500.)

Practical Kabbalah is one way of dealing with evil. It is a form of magic, the dangerous art of gaining power over the psychological (Yeziratic) World through the use of symbols; but some rabbis have considered it to be legitimate if scrupulously applied. In the course of time such practices became corrupt and gave Kabbalah a dubious reputation. The validity of the techniques remains, however, in that certain exercises can bring about deep changes in consciousness and remove psychological problems that in earlier times were seen in terms of demonic intrusion. (Amulet against the evil eye, Netherlands, 17th c.)

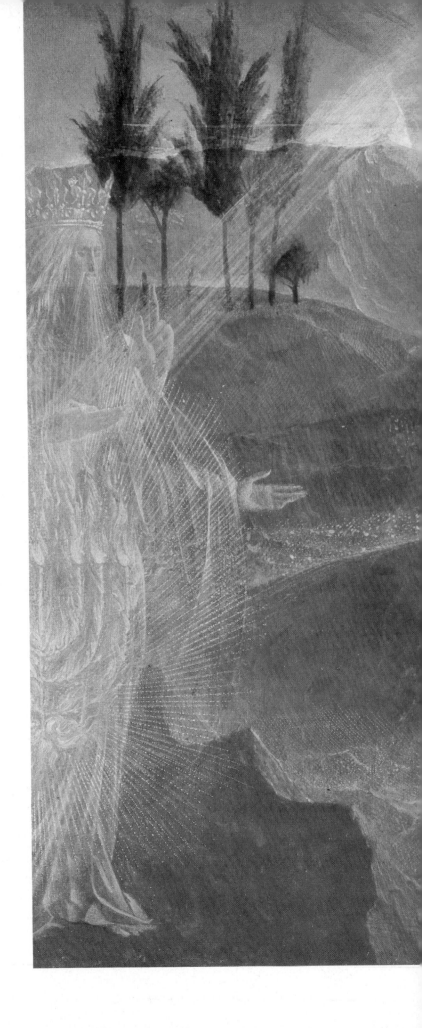

The closest most people come to the subject of this book is the one sublime experience in everyone's life. Such a moment may occur under any circumstances, but its quality is always the same. A heightened physical awareness changes into a psychological lucidity which then transforms into a profound consciousness of the totality of the universe and the Presence of Divinity. One is in direct contact with all the Worlds at once, and perceives both the complexity and the unity of everything. Although the moment may last just one second, it is always unforgettable. It is the gift of Heaven; and, if one wishes to take up the option of initiation, it can be the door into the inner and upper kingdoms. Here Moses experiences such a moment. His is the choice to bring the enslaved children of Israel – the psyche, with its mass of discontent and engrained habit – into the promised land or spiritual World of Creation; or to remain, unrealized, in a desert between the fleshpots of Egypt and the land flowing with milk and honey. (The Burning Bush, painting by Ernst Fuchs, Austria, 20th c.)

The first step in Kabbalah is to become familiar with the Sefirotic Tree. Without this key, little can be comprehended. To this end it is necessary to translate the nature of each Sefirah into human terms, so that the Divine image may be perceived in terms of man. The Tree is set out here in picture and story, through the works of Rembrandt (who was himself acquainted with Kabbalah). Malkhut, the Kingdom, is seen as the elemental physical body. Yesod, the Foundation of the ego, is expressed in the figure of the gifted but wilful son, Absalom, who sought to be king. Hod, Reverberation, is the mercurial part of our natural intelligence, which learns and communicates; Nezah, Eternity, is the sphere of instinctual cycles and the preoccupation with pleasure and pain. Tiferet, Beauty, is the self that watches all, and wrestles with the angel over the issue of My Will and Thy Will. Gevurah is the emotional quality of Judgment, discipline and decision; it complements Hesed, the emotional tendency to Mercy, love and forgiveness. The non-Sefirah of Daat is the voice of the unseen, imparting Knowledge from beyond this world. Binah is the intellectual capacity for Understanding through long reflection; Wisdom, Hokhmah, is embodied in the moment of revelation that bursts in upon the mind. There is no image of Keter, the Crown. The whole pattern of Attributes, with its relationships as set out in the paths of the Tree (p. 40), defines the anatomy of the psyche. (The Sefirot in human experience, seen through ten paintings by Rembrandt van Rijn, Netherlands, 17th c.)

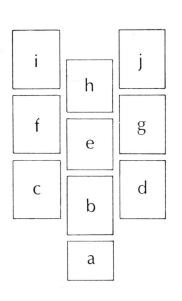

(a) Malkhut. The anatomy lesson of Dr Johan Deyman.
(b) Yesod. David and Absalom.
(c) Hod. The Artist's Son Titus at his Desk.
(d) Nezah. Saskia van Ulenborch in Arcadian Costume.
(e) Tiferet. Jacob (Israel) Wrestling with the Angel.
(f) Gevurah. Man in a Golden Helmet.
(g) Hesed. Head of an Old Rabbi.
(h) Daat. St Matthew and the Angel.
(i) Binah. St Anastasius.
(j) Hokhmah. Belshazzar's Feast.

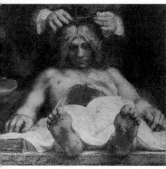

Next page:
The opening word of Genesis, Bereshith, is said to be the root of the whole Teaching. In reading the Bible, Kabbalists use a variety of methods of interpretation – literal, allegorical or metaphysical – but the aim is always that of opening what are called the seven gates of comprehension. The first three are those of everyday action, feeling and thinking; the latter four involve inner awakening, awareness of the soul, and spiritual consciousness, leading to the Divine Presence. (They correspond to the triads of the Tree of the Kabbalistic Way seen on p. 22.) At each of these stages the text of the Bible takes on a new meaning, so that the symbol of Adam and Eve, for example, takes on in turn a physical, psychological and spiritual reality. (Opening page of Hebrew Bible with pictorial summary of the whole biblical narrative, Germany, c. 1300.)

One of the most potent symbols in the Bible is the Crossing of the Red Sea. This is not just the record of a miraculous event in a nation's history but the description of a spiritual initiation. Once an aspirant has left the old way of life, represented by Egypt, and crossed the sea of commitment, he cannot go back. He has to face the inner psychological desert, with its rebellions and its discipline, its purification and its revelation on an inner Mount Sinai, until the old slave psychology has died and he is ready in a new generation of attitudes to enter the promised land of the spirit. (The Crossing of the Red Sea, ms. illumination by Belbello da Pavia, Italy, 15th c.)

53

סדר
הגדה של פסח
עם פירוש יפה וציורים נאים מהאותיות
והמופתים שעשה הקבה לאבותינו
ונוסף
על זה כל המסעות במדבר עד
חלוקת הארץ לכל שבטה
ישראל : וצורת בית
המקדש ותבב אכר
חרות
על לוחת נהושת ש הבחור
כמר אברם בר יעקב
כמשפחת אברהם אבינו
בבית ובמצות האלוף
כהרר משה וויזל יצו
אשר ארם מצא חכמה
והורני דרך במלכת הקדש

נדפס
באמשטרדם
בשנת ברוך אברם לאל עליון קנה שמים וארץ לפק

Kabbalistic instruction can come in many ways. It can be imparted in a formal manner in a school or be given individually in conversation, by demonstration, or in ritual. There is no rule except that the pupil be mature and capable of receiving instruction. The theory of Kabbalah may, for instance, be privately or publicly taught through a ceremony such as the Passover, so that its inner meaning – of being ready to leave the house of bondage – becomes directly relevant. In these first years the system has to be thoroughly learnt; and this tuition may come from a rabbi or from someone who outwardly appears the least qualified of people but who inwardly has a connection with the tradition. (Frontispiece showing the upper Sefirot, the lower Sefirot being in the reader, Haggadah, Netherlands, 17th c.)

Theory is complemented by practice. Here esoteric ideas are interwoven with the cycle of Jewish festivals and the major events of life. Each day has its phases of Mercy, Grace and Severity, each week its Sefirotic progression, each season its spiritual significance. In life every stage is part of a sacred journey. The rites of circumcision, Barmitzvah and marriage complete the natural cycle before the inner growth of the soul and the development of the spirit become the focus of existence. (Kabbalistic practice, lithograph, France, 19th c.)

To the Kabbalist, practice must never become routine. While he may outwardly perform exactly the same procedure as his co-religionists, he seeks to remain aware of the inner content of what he is doing in relation to himself, the universe and God. His intention, or Kavvanah, is consciously directed, because he knows that what he is doing will have an effect on the whole of existence. He accepts the responsibility of will, and operates according to his knowledge of the upper Worlds,

so that a simple ceremony becomes a focus for a Divine influx. (A mizrah, or menorah, for orienting prayer in time and space, Iran, 19th c.)

A relationship with an instructor is necessary in the early stages of Kabbalah. A teacher not only imparts knowledge but watches over the student, standing in for the latter's still imperfectly developed self consciousness. In this way the student learns to observe his own nature objectively and to receive, through

merit on his part and Grace from above, the blessing that comes down and through the teacher. This can occur only if the teacher himself is a person of inner knowledge and has direct connection with the middle and upper Sefirot of the Tree of the Tradition (see p. 83). Such a mentor has to have deep psychological insight and personal experience of the spiritual and Divine Worlds. (The Teacher, page from Maimonides' *Guide to the Perplexed*, ms., Spain, 14th c.)

There are three initial approaches in Kabbalah, which correspond to body, heart and head. These are the methods of action, devotion and contemplation: the literal, allegorical and metaphysical approaches to religious tradition (see pp. 80–85).

Action is the approach of ritual, be it a communal ceremony or a private practice. A daily task can

become an act of worship, whether inside or outside the rituals of orthodoxy: the criterion is that the action be dedicated and filled with a consciousness of the Divine within physical reality.

Devotion may take many forms. It can be in prayer or in service or in anything that has the heart as its prime mover. Love and fear of God is its motivation: it creates a deep sense of gratitude for what is given, and obedience to Divine intention.

Contemplation is the approach of the mind. It is the use of the intellect to penetrate and comprehend the universe at its deepest level. Such reflections may examine the latest stage of cosmic evolution, or the long-term destiny of the spirit, or the current situation within the Divine plan. (Action: The Synagogue in Livorno on Simchas Torah, painting by S. A. Hart, 19th c.; left. Devotion: The Blessing over the Candles, painting by Isidor Kaufmann, 19th c.; below. Contemplation: The Last Prayer, painting by Samuel Hirschenberg, 19th c.; below left.)

After action, devotion and contemplation, all of which form part of the aspiring Kabbalist's work, the fourth approach – that of mystical perception – comes as the first stage in real Kabbalistic experience. In this there is a breakthrough, out of the natural into the supernatural Worlds above, where the Kabbalist sees what is usually hidden from the eye – such as the radiance about living things – or converses with long-dead teachers, or even sees the angelic beings about the Throne of Heaven. However, such prophetic experience is fraught with danger if the individual is untrained or immature. (Vision of Isaiah, from ms. Book of Isaiah, Reichenau, Germany, 11th c.)

The highest level of human achievement is direct contact with the Divine. This may come about through the merit of hard spiritual work or through Grace from above. Such contact, however momentary, has always been considered the crown of a life. It is the duty and privilege of the Kabbalist to strive for the Divine connection through the practice of Devekut, cleaving to God, in a constant act of remembrance of the Divine Presence. (Moses speaks with God, from ms. Haggadah, Spain, 13th c.)

The purpose of self unification is to aid in the integration of the four Worlds. In this way, existence is brought closer to its full realization as the mirror of the Divine, into which the perfected Adam will gaze at the End of Days. This outward Work of Creation is symbolized here in a mezuzah, a prayer case made to be fixed to the door of a Jewish household. In this design, it reminds those going in and out of Jacob's Ladder and the teaching of the four Worlds. (Mezuzah, Italy, 15th c.)

The vestments of the high priest are more than just decoration: they symbolize the four levels within a human being. The outer ephod, with its golden weave, represents the Divine part of a man (Azilut), with the blue surcoat as a heavenly or spiritual aspect (Beriah). The under garment represents the soul (Yezirah), and the priest's own body is the physical vehicle. The task of the Kabbalist is to bring all these levels into a harmonious unity, in order to become a being in whom – as in the high priest – the universe and Divinity are consciously manifest. (Aaron the high priest, statue, Netherlands, c. 1700.)

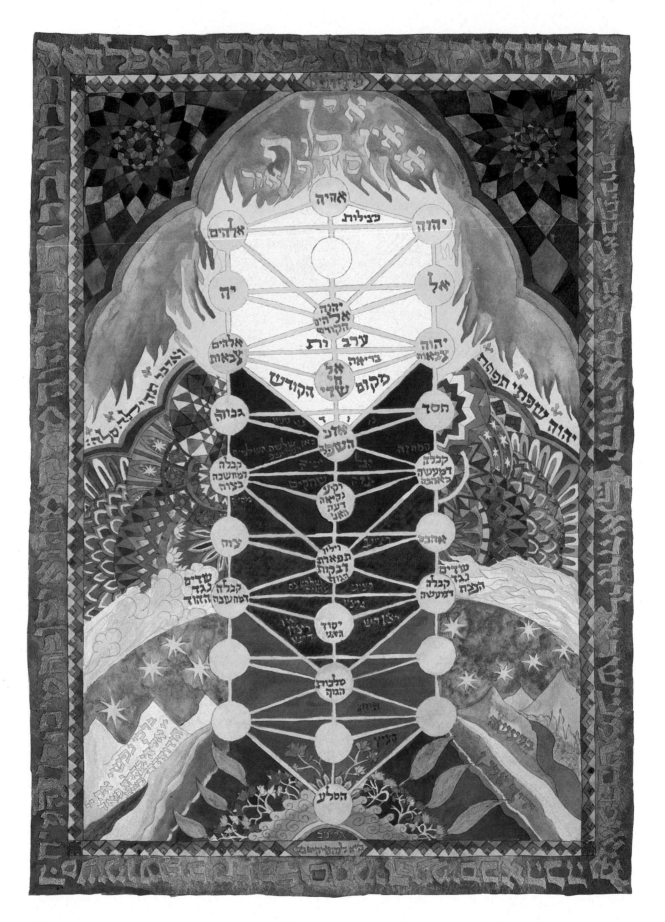

64

Themes

The Tree of Holy Fruit, as it is sometimes called, has been arranged in many different ways according to the Kabbalistic school involved. Here the paths focus on the place of Knowledge, while on either side and below subsidiary systems develop the metaphysical view of Isaac Luria (see pp. 72–73). (Sefirotic system according to *Pa'amon ve-Rimmon*, Amsterdam, 1708.)

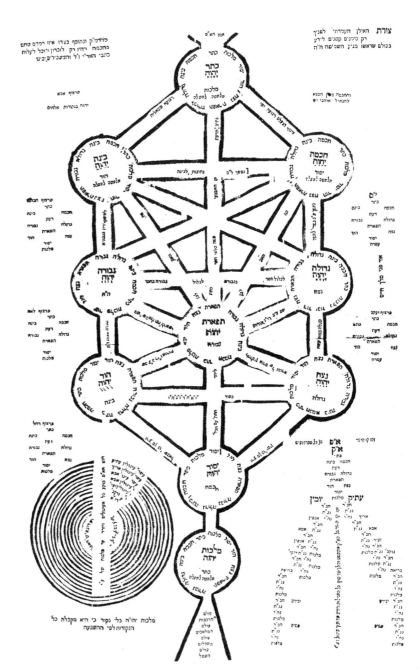

Facing page:

Before perfection is reached, there are many stages to pass. There may be glimpses of the way ahead, but not a step may be missed if the innocent soul which descends into this world is to become the experienced spirit which reaches journey's end in reunion with the Divine. This Jacob's Ladder drawn by a modern American Kabbalist sets out the successive stages of ascent through the Worlds, including the obstacles to be overcome, such as wilfulness and will-lessness. When willingness is achieved, the individual submits to Heaven. Then I and Thou are in union and the Divine Will is done. (The Way of Perfection.)

the Name of God and the Hebrew letters are related to Greek and Babylonian concepts of the principles that govern the universe. At the centre is the Tetragrammaton, YHVH, arranged in the form of the Tetractys of Pythagoras $(1+2+3+4=10)$ and marked at the corners by the 3 mother letters, those of air, water and fire. The circles show the remaining 19 letters of the Hebrew alphabet arranged to correspond to the 7 planets and 12 zodiacal signs. Contrary to certain widely held preconceptions about Kabbalah, it has remained open to contemporary ideas in every age. (Diagram from Sefer Yezirah, the Book of Formation, Babylonia, c. 6th c.)

Right:
With the transfer of the esoteric line from the declining Babylonian schools to Europe in the tenth century came major changes. By the fourteenth century, Kabbalah had been transformed from an exclusive study into a general one, and was known to many of the intelligentsia of the time, including Christian scholars. Despite orthodox opposition, it expressed itself in religious practice, metaphysics, science, literature and even art, as seen here in a Tree composed of words. This was a golden age of innovation and proliferation. (Calligraphic diagram of the Tree from ms., France, 13th c. Bibliothèque Nationale, Paris.)

Changing forms of Kabbalah

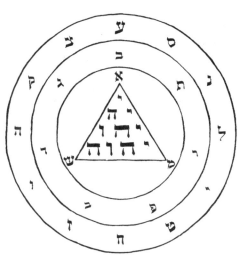

The oldest mystical text is the Torah, the Pentateuch or five books of Moses. Based on tribal myth and saga, history and Divine revelation, the scriptures form a many-levelled body of literature, designed to be understood esoterically as well as practically. The Torah (or Book of Instruction) became the outer aspect of a spiritual tradition that was imparted in full only to those who sought its deeper meaning. (Sefer Torah, or Scroll of the Law, ms., Jewish Museum, London.)

Between the later biblical and post-Temple periods (6th century BCE – 6th century CE), Jewish mystics drew much influence from the cultures which surrounded them. Out of this came an amalgam of metaphysical systems. Here

Right, below:
By the eighteenth century many changes had occurred within the tradition, and, in the hands of the successors of Isaac Luria (see pp. 72–73, 77), it became extremely complex. In Eastern Europe this led to oversimplifications which, among the unlearned, turned into a belief in wonder-working saints with supernatural powers (here expressed through the hands, the traditional symbol of blessing). This generated a reaction among the orthodox, who saw profound ideas being debased. The assimilated Jews of the West, perceiving only the medieval image of the tradition and its contemporary degeneracy, regarded Kabbalah as superstitious and irrelevant to life in an Age of Reason. (Hands inscribed with Kabbalistic symbols from *Shefa Tal* by Shabbetai Horowitz, Poland, 1712.)

After the eighteenth- and nineteenth-century Age of Reason, in which the tradition went underground, or was maintained only by the most orthodox of Jews, the twentieth century has brought a revival of interest in Kabbalah. In its traditional form it is studied both as an academic subject and as part of a movement towards spiritual regeneration. It is also practised, both inside and outside orthodox Judaism, by groups all over the world who seek to relate its eternal principles to contemporary conditions and knowledge, just as their predecessors did in medieval Spain and ancient Babylon. (A modern Kabbalistic view of the earth in relation to man and the solar system, after Halevi, *Tree of Life*.)

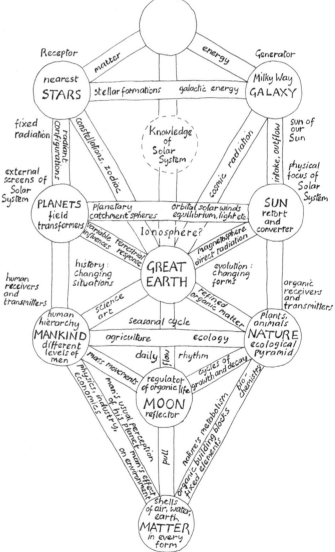

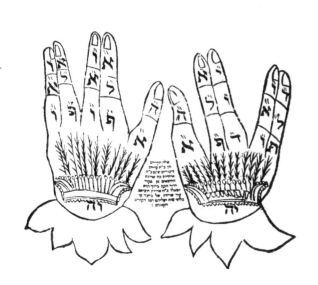

The Name of God (יהוה) in illuminated border with Hebrew text.

Views of eternity

YHVH, the Shem ha-Meforash or Tetra-grammaton, the four-letter Name of God, is the most often used symbol for Divinity. It contains in its letters and forms all the powers of Eternity and the Will to sustain it as long as God wills. Should the Most Holy One cease to want the World of Emanation to exist, we and all the universe would vanish. (The Name of God from Bible in Sefardi hand, 1385. British Library, London.)

The likeness of a man (Ezekiel 1:26) was used by early mystics to describe the Divine Glory. The figure of a primordial, Azilutic man, God's image, is the embodiment of the Sefirot. This, the most perfect image of Divinity, is seen not as God but as His reflection, and therefore a representation of him does not contravene the Second Command-ment. Azilut, the Divine World of Emanation, is not God but His garment of Light. (Adam Kadmon, Primordial Man, showing the Sefirot.)

The Divine World of the Sefirot has been defined in many ways. Here the initial letters of all the Sefirot have been placed in order, with Keter the Crown enclosing the rest and Malkhut the King-dom at the centre. This is probably based on the allegorical idea that the Sefirot are nutshells and kernels one within the other. The model also illus-trates the all-enclosing Absolute, which holds everything in its place according to an archetypal sequence. (Diagram from *Pardes Rimmonim* by Moses Cordovero, Cracow, 1592.)

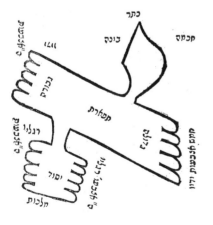

The Hebrew letter Alef is not only the first letter of the alphabet but the initial of Azilut, the World of Emanation. Its form is perceived by some Kabbalists as a diagram of the Sefirot (with Tiferet at the centre) and of the body of Adam Kadmon, whose fingers and toes can be seen on each side and below. (Alef from *Pardes Rimmonim* by Moses Cordovero, Cracow, 1592.)

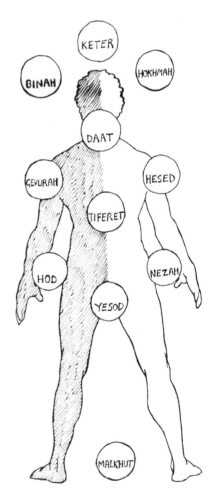

Adam Kadmon figure with the Sefirot: KETER, BINAH, HOKHMAH, DAAT, GEVURAH, HESED, TIFERET, HOD, NEZAH, YESOD, MALKHUT.

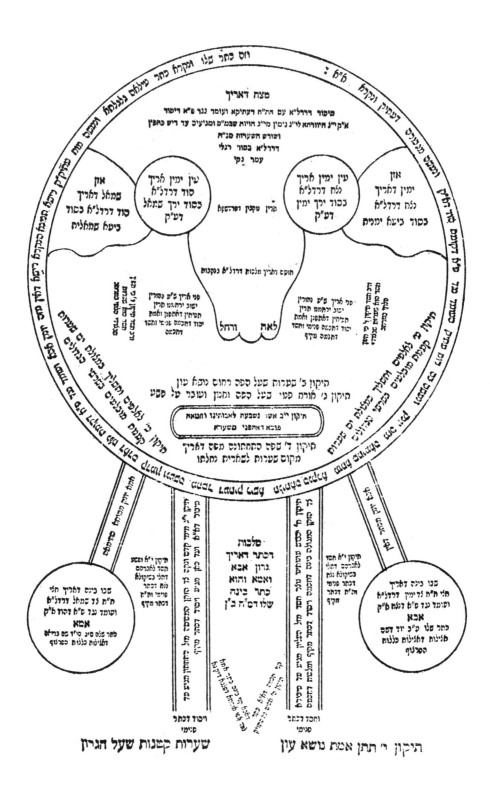

The face of Adam Kadmon was used by later Kabbalists as a metaphor of the Mercy through which Divine radiance emanated. This was taken further in some systems in that the divisions of the beard and the geometry of the features defined the relationships between the Sefirot. Below this Long (long-suffering or merciful) Face was the Short Face which expressed the more rigorous aspect of the Divine. (Face of the Long One, detail of Lurianic scheme, Poland, 19th c. See pp. 72–73.)

69

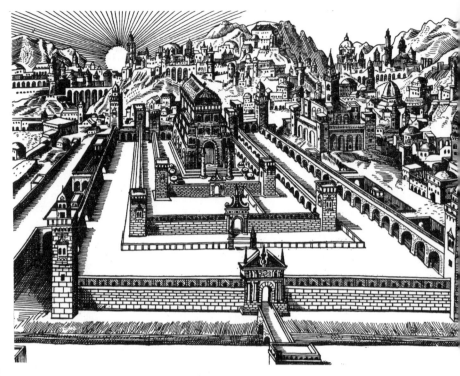

Four levels of existence

The Temple of Jerusalem, shown here in an idealized view, expresses the notion of the four Worlds that compose existence. The lower three levels are the physical, psychological and spiritual planes of the universe. The Temple building itself is the Divine level, with its twin pillars at the entrance, beyond which ten Menorot (see p. 36), one for each Sefirah, stand before the innermost level, the Holy of Holies. (The Temple from Haggadah, Amsterdam, 1695.)

The design for the Tabernacle, given to Moses on Sinai, contains the arrangement of the four Worlds within its plan (see p. 93). The space between the Cherubim above the ark is the upper part of the Divine; the Ark itself is the lower, and so on. The ranks of high priest, priest, Levite and Israelite correspond to the four human levels of Divinity, spirit, soul and body. (Tabernacle plan.)

Within Azilut, the Divine World of Emanation, are four levels: those of Will, Intellect, Emotion and Action. These in turn are manifested in the unfolding of existence out of Azilut (itself the realm of Will) into the lower Worlds of Beriah (Intellect), Yezirah (Emotion) and Asiyyah (Action). This scheme is often expressed in the decorative finials that cap the scrolls of the Torah. The crown represents the Divine World, with the three steps as the separated Worlds of Creation, Formation and Action. (A Rimmon or finial, England, 1767. Jewish Museum, London.)

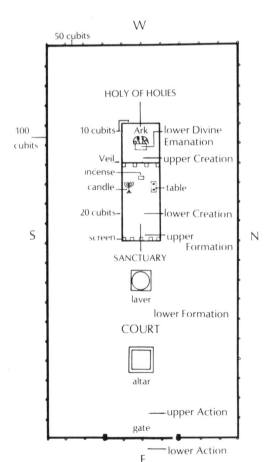

W

50 cubits

HOLY OF HOLIES

100 cubits

10 cubits — Ark — lower Divine Emanation

Veil — upper Creation

incense

candle — table

20 cubits — lower Creation

S — N

screen — upper Formation

SANCTUARY

laver

lower Formation

COURT

altar

upper Action

gate

lower Action

E

The four Holy Living Creatures of Ezekiel 1 and the Book of Revelation are symbols of the four Worlds. The human form is Adam Kadmon (p. 68), the fiery and Divine domain of Emanation; the eagle, the airy level of cosmic Creation; the lion, the watery level of the heart or Formation and the bull, the earthy level of the natural World of Action. In the centre is the Messiah, in accordance with an ancient Jewish conception (see pp. 88–89), surrounded by angelic beings and the souls of the righteous. (Tympanum of Saint-Trophime, Arles, France, 12th c.)

To the four Worlds, Kabbalists add a fifth level, the realm of the Kelippot or shells, better known as Hell. This dark side of existence is seen here as having seven levels of suffering or uncleanness, where those who go against the Will of God remain, half in and half out of evolution, until they repent – or until, as the only truly dead, they are resurrected at the End of Days. (Gehennah, detail of Last Judgment fresco attributed to Andrea Orcagna and Nardo, Camposanto, Pisa, Italy, 14th c.)

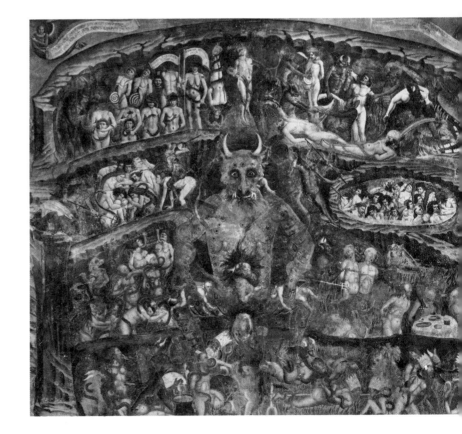

Alternative systems

Of all the many systems that exist within Kabbalah, the most commonly known is the Lurianic scheme. Its basis was the work of Isaac Luria, who lived in sixteenth-century Palestine, at the Kabbalistic centre of Safed. Evil, as Luria saw it, was the result of ancient events in Azilut, the highest World, where the seven lowest Sefirot, unable to contain the flow of Divinity, shattered, causing the Worlds below to sink beneath their true level. He saw the redemption of man as a participation in the work of Tikkun, the restitution of the universe through the reorganization of its Sefirotic system. Thus good actions here below would help to eliminate evil in the Worlds above. This notion had a great appeal to a Jewish community that was still in shock from the expulsion from Spain in 1492. Luria's system largely displaced all others, although his disciples developed widely differing versions of his ideas.

The scroll reproduced here sets out one complex scheme (right to left). In it, concepts that predate Luria have been incorporated into a post-Lurianic arrangement which by the nineteenth century had become intelligible only to the learned. Ordinary people did, however, take to heart such concepts as that of the sparks of Divinity buried in everyday things, and set out to redeem these 'hidden lights' as a way of Kabbalah in action. The popularity of Luria's world-view has led many to accept it as the mainstream of Kabbalah, when in fact it is an innovation and one of several alternative schemes. (Scroll of Trees, Poland, 19th c. Alfred Cohen Collection.)

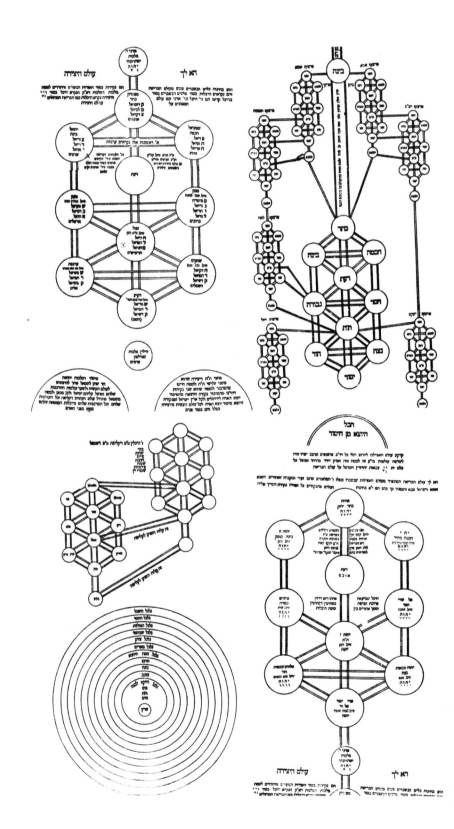

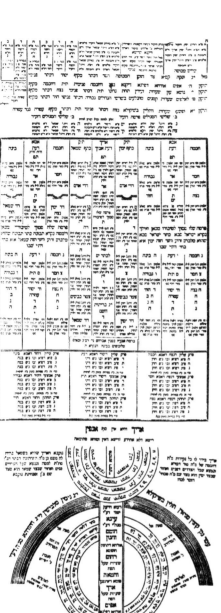

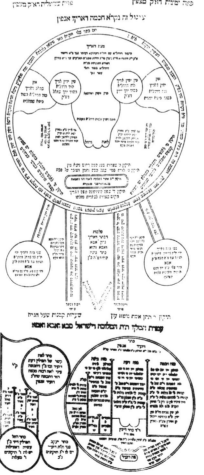

Creation, from top to bottom, is filled with creatures. The Tachutonim, those who dwell below, do not usually perceive those who dwell above, the Elyonim; however, the presence of supernatural creatures can sometimes be felt in sacred places, where the ordinary level of consciousness is raised. (Cherubim hovering over the ark of the tabernacle, from ms., France, 13th c. British Library, London.)

The nature of angelic creatures is said to be like that of creatures below, except that they have no physical functions and no individual will. Because of this they are in their Worlds as incomplete as plants or animals, and have little notion of human affairs. They carry out the routine work of the upper Worlds, but as the agents of Divinity they may not act outside their express function. (Seraph, carved relief, Syria, 6th c.)

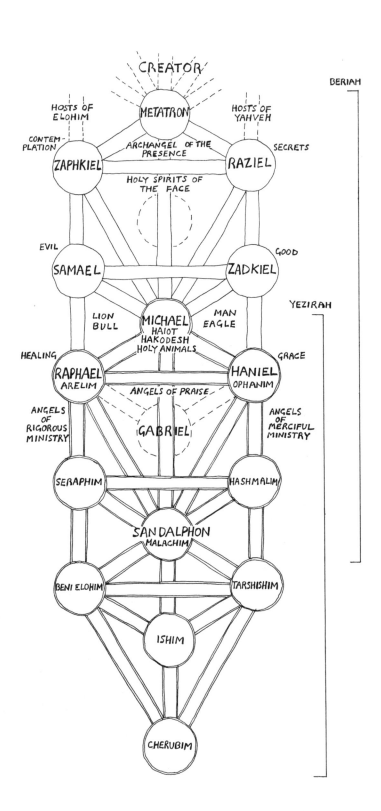

74

Left:
The hierarchy of angelic beings conforms to the order of the Worlds. In Genesis 1, the fowl of the air are the archangels of Beriah or Creation, while the fish of the sea are the angels of Yezirah or Formation. According to tradition each World is divided into its own hierarchy of levels and Pillars. The highest entities of the angelic World of Creation are the holy spirits of the inner council, under Metatron; on the central Pillar the great archangels Michael and Gabriel hold special roles in relation to man in that they are vehicles of Grace through which the Divine Metatron communicates to Sandalphon at the level of man (at the Tiferet or self of the psyche). (Angelic and archangelic hierarchy, after Halevi, *A Kabbalistic Universe*.)

Lucifer, the Bringer of Light, was one of the highest of the archangels; but when he refused to submit himself to Adam – as even Michael, the Captain of the Hosts, had done – he was given the odious title of Samael, God's Poisoner, the destructive aspect of Divine Judgment (Gevurah) and the leader of the demonic hosts which test Creation. But even Lucifer, who is also Satan, the tester of man, may be redeemed at the End of Days in just proportion to his state of submission. (Satan falling, engraving by Gustave Doré from *Paradise Lost* by John Milton, France, 19th c.)

The battle between good and evil within the human soul is watched over by angels and demons. Every person, Kabbalists say, has one of each hovering over him as he makes his moral choices; at the end of life one or the other claims its victory and takes the soul to its abode above or below. Seen in modern terms, this is the manifestation of the dark and light psychological archetypes; the unconscious or post-mortem states may only be speculated upon, or experienced by those sensitive to the levels of reality on which these archetypes operate. (Demons and angels battle for human souls, detail of fresco attributed to Francesco Traini, Camposanto, Pisa, Italy, 14th c.)

Miracles and magic

The difference between miracles and magic is that they operate from different Worlds. The miraculous is the Will of Heaven, ordained in Beriah, the spiritual World of Creation; magic is the application of human will at the psychological level of Yezirah, the World of Formation. Acting under the Will of God, Moses excelled the magical prowess of the Egyptian priests (Exodus 7). The snake forms they had conjured were eaten by that created by God through Moses. (Moses' staff turned into a serpent, from Haggadah, Spain, 14th c. British Library, London.)

The miraculous is cosmic in scale, although it may work through the life of an individual. It changes the course of great events or intervenes to transform an ordinary situation into a heaven-sent opportunity. (The sun stands still for Joshua, painting by John Martin, England, 19th c. United Grand Lodge of England.)

Many stories of miracles and magic are based on real but essentially spiritual or psychological events which have been allegorized to make a teaching point and then made literal by gossip. Rabbi Naphtali Cohen of Frankfurt am Main made the sun come out, metaphorically, in the benighted mind of one of his students. This story was taken as physical fact by ignorant people who saw Kabbalah as magic, and so, when the Ghetto was burnt down in 1711, Naphtali got the blame. (Naphtali Cohen bringing the sun out at night by his Kabbalistic powers, engraving, 19th c.)

Practical or magical Kabbalah has never been approved of by orthodox opinion, but it has nevertheless always been practised. There are many Kabbalistic books based on the fact that human will can manipulate psychological principles and thereby control conditions in the World of Formation and achieve, in certain circumstances, the materialization of a willed object. Such operations are traditionally carried out through the invocation of angelic or Divine names in a ritual form with a clearly stated aim. Shown here is a formula for conjuring up a spirit which shall submit to the direction of the magician. Such operations, if ever necessary, may be carried out only after Divine assent has been asked. (Angelic seal from the so-called Sixth Book of Moses, Germany, 18th c.)

Most practical Kabbalistic operations are preventative. Here an amulet acts as protection against pestilence. It was designed by a pupil of the great Isaac Luria, who, like many others in the sixteenth century and earlier, saw such amulets as a legitimate defence against unseen hazards. Disease was one of these hazards, and was widely interpreted as an attack by demonic forces. The words and symbols used here are a blend of Kabbalistic and Gentile magical formulae. This magical adulteration of the tradition was to discredit Kabbalah in the eyes of the Jews who had obtained a Western education. (Amulet from *Shaar ha-Yihud* by Hayyim Vital, 16th c.)

The traditional objection to magic, on the part of many Kabbalists, is that it alters the balance of the Worlds, putting things out of their proper order. Magic is also seen as an obstruction to spiritual development, in that a magician becomes so entangled in the World of Yezirah that he cannot enter the Worlds above. Moreover, the use of the Divine Names for any but sacred actions is considered blasphemous. And yet, despite its obviously degenerate features, Kabbalistic magic has often been practised with good intentions and in a spirit of submission to God's Will. (Amulet to protect mother during childbirth, from *Book of Raziel*, Netherlands, 1701.)

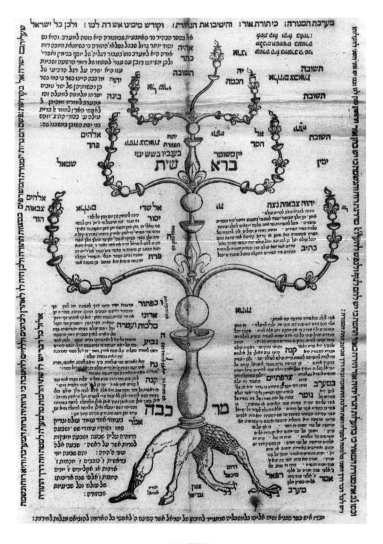

Christian and occult Kabbalah

Without question, much of what Joshua ben Miriam – otherwise Jesus of Nazareth – said came from the Jewish esoteric tradition of his time. Certainly, also, Saul of Tarsus – St Paul – was acquainted with the mystical line. Later, Kabbalah was transmitted in a Christian form by Jewish converts and by Christians who had studied with rabbis. This process reached its high point in the sixteenth century, when Kabbalist studies became fashionable among the European intelligentsia as source material for theological argument. This diagram of the Tree in the form of a Menorah is from a broadsheet by a Christian Kabbalist. (Detail of *Or Nerot ha-Menorah* by Guillaume Postel, Venice, 1548.)

The translation of Judaic into Christian Kabbalah was not a difficult process: the two religions share the same roots. The distinction lies in the role of the Messiah – the image of God in earthly man – whom Christians personify in Jesus of Nazareth. In this Christian adaptation of Kabbalah the outer circle of Ten Commandments represents the physical World of Asiyyah, the Hebrew alphabet the Formative World of Yezirah, the Sefirot (cloudy circle, clockwise from the top) the Creative World of Beriah, and the corresponding God Names (fiery circle) the Divine World of Azilut. At the centre is the Christ figure. This formulation stems from the Rosicrucians, a Christian mystical fraternity which emerged in the seventeenth century. (Christian Kabbalist diagram from *Amphitheatrum sapientiae aeternae solius versae* by Heinrich Khunrath, Hanover 1609.)

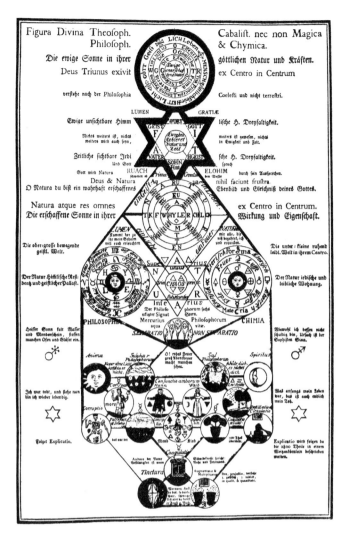

In this Rosicrucian interpretation of Kabbalah much of the symbolism has been buried in a mixture of magical, alchemical and Christian metaphysics. However, both scholars and initiates of the Western esoteric tradition owe much to the fragments of Kabbalah which still shine through corrupted texts and diagrams. (Figure of the Divine Kabbalistic, Magical, Philosophical and Chymical Theosophy from *Geheime Figuren der Rosenkreuzer*, Altona, 1785.)

The origin of Freemasonry is open to speculation; but its view of God, the universe and man shows clear affinities with that of the Kabbalists. Masons use the symbolism of Solomon's Temple, with its Pillars of Mercy and Severity; and the Masons who built the medieval European cathedrals made them into diagrams in stone on essentially Kabbalistic principles. (Frontispiece of *Masonic Miscellanies* by Stephen Jones, London, 1797.)

Occult Kabbalah has a history which goes back to Babylon. An outcrop of it manifested in medieval Europe in the design of the Tarot cards, from which modern playing-cards are derived. There is a suit for each World, composed of ten cards plus a page, knight, queen and king to indicate the four sub-levels. The occult feature of the system is the set of major trumps, twenty-two picture cards which relate to the paths on the Tree and the stages of evolution. Here Adam the Magician manipulates the symbols of the four Worlds while wearing the Hat of Eternity. (Tarot card, France, 16th c.)

Kabbalistic methods: action

Making ritual objects is an exercise of Kabbalistic action. Translating a spiritual idea, through a designed form, into a material symbol for use involves all the three lower Worlds. Here three crowns on a silver plate represent the supernal Sefirot of Keter, Hokhmah and Binah; the Pillars are those of Severity and Mercy; the seven bells symbolize the seven lower Sefirot of Construction. The plate is hung round the Sefer Torah (p. 34) when it is not being read. (Silver 'breastplate', Germany, 1680. Jewish Museum, London.)

The Passover festival is esoteric action in ritual form. The layout of the table and the symbolism of the service not only tell the story of the going out of Egypt but speak of the inner preparation for the journey to the promised land of the spirit. Everyone present is enjoined to consider himself as one of the Israelites ready to set out on the Way. (Passover dish, Hungary, 17th c. Wolfson Museum, Jerusalem.)

On most days the orthodox Jew puts on the phylacteries or Tefilin. These are ritual objects containing sacred texts which are bound on to the head and arm in a formal manner. The performance of this action brings the body, heart and mind into consciousness of God; every stage of the ritual, such as the binding on of the straps to form the inital letter of a Divine Name, is done with deep inner concentration. (The Tefilin and their application from *Cérémonies et coûtumes religieuses . . .* by B. Picart, 1733.)

Left, below:

The human body is a clear expression of Sefirotic law in the physical World. It has four levels of mechanical, chemical, electronic and conscious activity. The side Pillars, in the World of Asiyyah, are energy and matter, with the axis of will in the centre. Tiferet is the central nervous system, with the autonomic at Yesod. At Malkhut are the skin and bones of solid matter; with liquids, gases and heat this makes up the four levels of Action in the flesh. 'If you want to know what is Above, then look Below,' said one Kabbalist. This system is set out in diagrammatic form on p. 15; the schema shown here uses the analogue of a house to demonstrate not only corresponding organs and functions but the four elemental levels in the flesh which correspond to the four Worlds. (The house of the Body from *Maaseh Tobiyyah* by Tobias Cohn, 1707.)

This page:

In Hebrew the word Avodah means both work and worship. Its use in Kabbalah expresses the combined and conscious intent that goes into every action; everything outwardly done has an inner content which makes the act itself sacred. In this way the upper and lower Worlds meet and are unified in the Kavvanah, or conscious intent of work. Here a calligrapher writes the scroll of the Law: a most perfect livelihood. (Scribe at work, Jerusalem, 20th c.)

The principles summarized in the Tree have their application through all the Worlds, in everything that functions as an organism or organization – even a motor car. At Hokhmah and Binah are the ideas behind the machine, its invention and design; at Hesed and Gevurah the mechanical principles of Force and Form, propulsion and regulation; at Nezah and Hod the active and passive operational functions. On the central Pillar is seen the material base (Malkhut), as affected by the look and behaviour of the car (Yesod) and the will of the driver (Tiferet). To perceive the Sefirot at work in a machine or any human artefact is to comprehend Law at work in the lowest World, as man exerts his will to create like his maker. (The motor car and the Sefirotic Tree.)

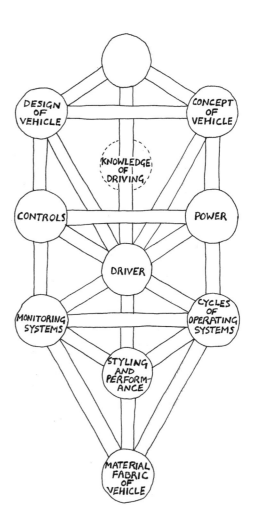

Kabbalistic methods: devotion

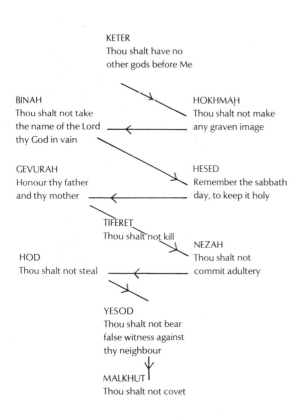

KETER
Thou shalt have no
other gods before Me

BINAH
Thou shalt not take
the name of the Lord
thy God in vain

HOKHMAH
Thou shalt not make
any graven image

GEVURAH
Honour thy father
and thy mother

HESED
Remember the sabbath
day, to keep it holy

TIFERET
Thou shalt not kill

HOD
Thou shalt not steal

NEZAH
Thou shalt not
commit adultery

YESOD
Thou shalt not bear
false witness against
thy neighbour

MALKHUT
Thou shalt not covet

The way of devotion begins with love and fear of God and is embodied in the ten Commandments. These are based upon the Sefirot, with the first three relating to the supernal or Divine triad. The fourth and fifth, at Hesed and Gevurah, speak of devotion and respect at the emotional level; those below, which refer to external matters, must additionally be seen as guides to inner practice: thus, one must not kill the self or its hope of spiritual growth (Murder, Tiferet), adulterate the spiritual life through power-seeking (Adultery, Nezah), misuse acquired knowledge to steal unfair advantage (Theft, Hod), delude oneself or others through the Yesodic ego, or covet possession of anything in the universe: all is God's Kingdom (Malkhut). (The Ten Commandments, Sefirotic correspondences.)

'Blessed art Thou, O Lord our God, king of the universe, Who bringest forth bread from the earth.' This prayer of thanks is one of the blessings that are recited by the devout Jew on all the occasions of life: there are blessings upon seeing lightning, or the sea, or a wise man; blessings for wine or for good health. These devotions draw attention to the truth that everything emanates from the Divine; the worshipper seeks to recall this awareness in whatever he sees or does. The daily repetition of such prayers must never be mere lip-service. (The prayer of thanksgiving for bread, calligraphy, 20th c. Joseph Russell Collection.)

Many books have been written by Kabbalists on the Way of Devotion. They give instructions on right conduct and ethical practice as well as various techniques of prayer and submission to God's Will. The eleventh-century Spanish Jew Bahya ibn Pakudah (who originally wrote his *Duties of the Heart* in Arabic) dwells upon conscience, humility and asceticism as well as emphasizing the inward observance of the Law in grateful response to the benefits bestowed by God's love. (Title page of a Ladino, or Judaeo-Spanish, edition of *Hovot ha-Levavot*, by Bahya ibn Pakudah, Venice 1713.)

Next page:
Abraham Abulafia, who lived in the thirteenth century, was a strange man even by visionary standards. Part prophet, part metaphysician and part poet, he devised a technique of meditation which dislocated the ordinary (Yesodic) mind so that the heart might comprehend what was happening during prayer. By these 'circles of instruction', and the continual recombining of the Hebrew letters and Names, the meditator sought to transcend the rational and so perceive supernatural realms. The method is not dissimilar to certain mantra practices of the East. (Instructions for meditation from ms. of Abulafia's writings.)

Above right:
The relationship between the Patriarchs can be symbolically understood by reference to the Sefirot: David stands at Malkhut, Joseph at Yesod; Moses and Aaron at Nezah and Hod; Jacob (Israel) at Tiferet. Abraham and Isaac, at Hesed and Gevurah, epitomize the relationship between love and fear, with Abraham's

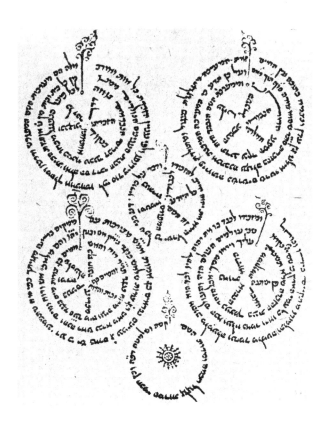

obedience on Mount Moriah (Genesis 22) as the ultimate act of sacrifice. His offering of that which is most precious to him is met by heavenly intervention, as the soul is touched by the Divine. (Silver gilt dish for the ceremony of Redemption of the Firstborn, Austria, 19th c. Jewish Museum, London.)

The first stages of Kabbalistic training are concerned with learning to submit the heart. This requires both discipline and love, as several levels of will have to be conquered. The love of the body, then ego love and self love, have to be identified and mastered. This leads, through devotion to a teacher, into a commitment to a tradition, which takes one from love of 'I' to love of 'Thou'. This approach develops compassion and discrimination, the qualities of the emotional or heart Sefirot of Hesed and Gevurah. (Stages of submission, after Halevi, *The Way of Kabbalah*.)

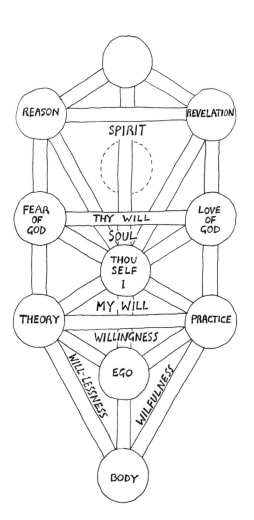

TABLE OF HEBREW AND CHALDEE LETTERS						
Number	Sound or Power	Hebrew and Chaldee Letters	Numerical Value	Roman character by which expressed in this work	Name	Signification of Name
1	a (soft breathing)	א	1 (Thousands are	A	Aleph	Ox
2	b, bh (v)	ב	2 denoted by a	B	Beth	House
3	g (hard), gh	ג	3 larger letter ;	G	Gimel	Camel
4	d, dh (flat th)	ד	4 thus an Aleph	D	Daleth	Door
5	h (rough breathing)	ה	5 larger than the	H	He	Window
6	v, u, o	ו	6 rest of the let-	V	Vau	Peg, nail
7	z, ds	ז	7 ters among	Z	Zayin	Weapon, sword
8	ch (guttural)	ח	8 which it is,	Ch	Cheth	Enclosure, fence
9	t (strong)	ט	9 signifies not 1,	T	Teth	Serpent
10	i, y (as in yes)	י	10 but 1000)	I	Yod	Hand
11	k, kh	כ Final = ך	20 Final = 500	K	Caph	Palm of the hand
12	l	ל	30	L	Lamed	Ox-goad
13	m	מ Final = ם	40 Final = 600	M	Mem	Water
14	n	נ Final = ן	50 Final = 700	N	Nun	Fish
15	s	ס	60	S	Samekh	Prop, support
16	O, aa, ng (gutt.)	ע	70	O	Ayin	Eye
17	p, ph.	פ Final = ף	80 Final = 800	P	Pe	Mouth
18	ts, tz, j	צ Final = ץ	90 Final = 900	Tz	Tzaddi	Fishing-hook
19	q, qh (guttur)	ק	100 (The finals are not	Q	Qoph	Back of the head
20	r	ר	200 always considered	R	Resh	Head
21	sh, s	ש	300 as bearing an in-	Sh	Shin	Tooth
22	th, t	ת	400 creased numeri-cal value)	Th	Tau	Sign of the cross

Gematria

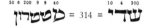

50 6 200   9 9 40   10 4 300

מטטרון = 314 = שדי

Metatron = 314 = Shaddai

Notarikon

תנ"ך = תורה . נביאים . כתובים

Torah + Neviim + Ketuvim = Tanakh
Pentateuch + Prophets + Hagiographa = Bible

Above:
If the prayer, 'Blessed art Thou O Lord our God, king of the universe, by Whose Word all things exist,' is contemplated word by word, then its full implication comes into consciousness. The saying of a blessing with intellectual awareness of its meaning is a technique which belongs to the method of contemplation. (Blessing to be said before eating certain food, calligraphy, 20th c. Joseph Russell Collection.)

Left:
The Hebrew letters, like those of many ancient alphabets, represent numbers and also symbols based on their pictographic origins. In the intellectual method of Gematria, when the numerical values of the letters of a word add up to the same total as those of another word, the words are related, to give insight into their meanings. Notarikon combines the initial letters of a phrase to give a new word, or reverses the process to reveal a sentence hidden within a word. (Hebrew alphabet, after Mathers, *The Kabbalah Unveiled*; examples of Gematria and Notarikon.)

Next page, above:
The contemplative method is particularly applicable to the study of metaphysics. Here the mind examines the structure and the processes of existence, with particular emphasis on the interaction of the Sefirot and their subsystems. The objective of such intellectual exercises is a religious one: to comprehend the mechanism by which Providence implements the Will of God. (Metaphysical scheme from *Kabbalah denudata* by Christian Knorr von Rosenroth, Frankfurt am Main, 1677.)

Above:
History reveals the state of the universe to the contemplative. In the Kabbalistic view the progress of mankind, and particularly that of the Jews, through time is the manifestation of Divine Will in action. No event is random; all are under Law. Israel was chosen to exemplify man's spiritual evolution, in that respect or neglect of the Teaching brings its consequences for the whole nation. As one rabbi said, 'The Jews are the first and the last in the world to be aware of good or bad times.' (Expulsion of the Jews from Prague, 1745, engraving, 18th c.)

Right:
The study of the letters of the Hebrew alphabet, with their corresponding numbers, their inner meanings, their shapes and their placing on the twenty-two paths of the Tree (see. p. 40), makes them keys to the understanding of Creation, which is said in esoteric literature to have come into being through their combination. Many schemes and systems have been devised, some profound and some superficial, according to the depth of the contemplation from which they arise. (Wheel of letters from *Pardes Rimmonim* by Moses Cordovero, Cracow, 1592.)

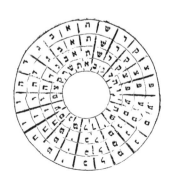

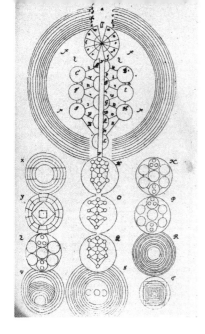

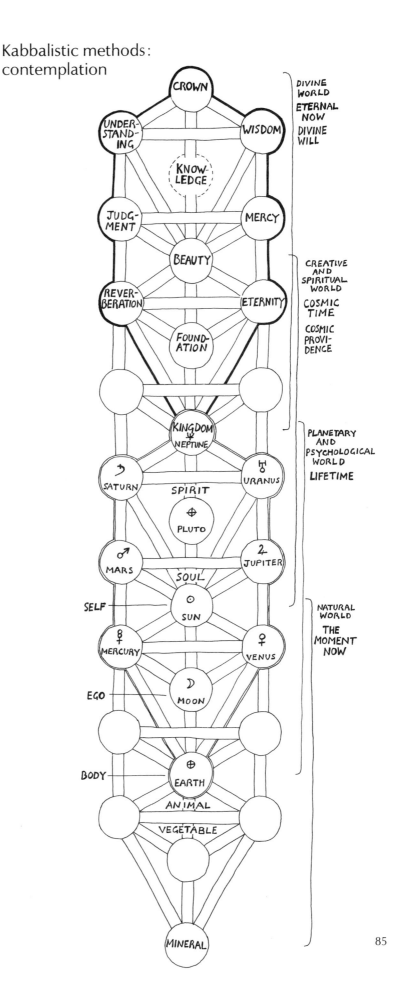

Kabbalistic methods: contemplation

DIVINE WORLD
ETERNAL NOW
DIVINE WILL

CREATIVE AND SPIRITUAL WORLD
COSMIC TIME
COSMIC PROVIDENCE

PLANETARY AND PSYCHOLOGICAL WORLD
LIFETIME

NATURAL WORLD
THE MOMENT NOW

Right:
The Divine Will creates the cosmic conditions that form the environment into which an individual is incarnated. Every human being, every place and every instant in time emanates from the Eternal Now of Azilut and manifests in the spiritual universe of Beriah; this in turn is the setting for the planets which, in the psychological World (Yezirah), correspond to the archetypal principles in the human psyche. The effect is seen in the World of Action (Asiyyah). In this way the Eternal Now is manifested in every present moment. (Providence and Time, after Kenton, *Anatomy of Fate*.)

Below:
The contemplation of universal events requires a knowledge of cosmic mechanisms. This includes astrology, despite a formal ban in the orthodox tradition. Rabbis used often to argue that Israel alone was above planetary influence. Israel here represents the higher state of human consciousness: only those who understand the Law that governs Creation can use their free will to place themselves above fate. (Jewish armillary sphere from *Maaseh Tobiyyah* by Tobias Cohn, 1707.)

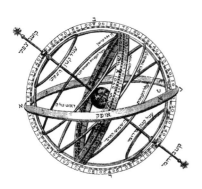

Death, rebirth, fate

Gilgulim, the cycles of reincarnation are an accepted part of Kabbalah. The transmigration of a soul over a series of lives is seen both as a learning process and as a way of carrying out a personal destiny or spiritual mission. Occasionally, through the misuse of free will, the mission may be set back for several lives – the Kabbalistic view of the Divine retribution 'unto the third and fourth [generation]' proclaimed in Exodus 20:5. Transmigration explains the common experience of people seeming already to know a person or place never seen before, and allows an apparent injustice to be corrected in the next life. (Death and rebirth: the old Jewish cemetery, Prague.)

The intrusion of a discarnate soul into the mind of a living person has been seen by many Kabbalists, and others, as the reality which underlies certain madnesses. The dead soul, which has returned to do unfinished business on earth, can be released through exorcism. The play *The Dybbuk*, by Shalom Anski, is based on this idea of a dead soul held back by an unfulfilled vow. (The possessed bride, a scene from *The Dybbuk*, performed by the Habimah Theatre, woodcut by Miron Sima, Jerusalem, 20th c.)

The ritual of a marriage is not simply a social event: it is a crossing of threads in the fabric of fate. Many strands bring the couple and their families together and spin their lives into a fabric that is woven on in their children. The interweaving of human fate is part of the cosmic curtain of destiny that hangs before the Throne of Heaven. All meetings and marryings are ordained to accomplish particular ends or prepare the way for others. (Nuptial ceremony of the Portuguese Jews from *Cérémonies et coûtumes religieuses ...* by B. Picart, 1733.)

Free will is everyone's right; but it is not often exercised to the full. A person may allow himself to be carried along by events, or he may forge his life by his own will; but even his will may still be no more than an unconscious drive. At the level of self consciousness, an individual acts through true choice. At a higher level still, one may act on spiritual rather than psychological criteria, making personal life a participation in cosmic life. Such men as Moses and Muhammad worked at this level of destiny. (Degrees of choice, after Kenton, *Anatomy of Fate*.)

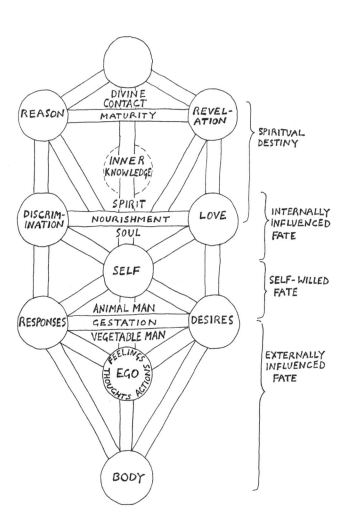

After death, according to Kabbalah, the human organism separates into its various distinct levels. As the Asiyyatic body disintegrates, the vital soul (the animal level of man) hovers for a while around the grave. The soul itself is taken into the World of Yezirah or Formation, where it contemplates its earthly performance and experiences paradise or purgatory. The Beriatic organism or spirit can, if sufficiently developed, ascend to the cosmic level of the World of Creation, until it descends, by necessity (Karma) or by choice, to return together with the soul to a fleshly body. (Paradise and Purgatory from ms. Simon Marmion Hours, France, 15th c. Victoria and Albert Museum, London.)

Masters and Messiahs

Enoch, the man who walked with God and was taken up into heaven without experiencing death, was transformed according to legend into the greatest of the archangels, Metatron, who bears the Name of God. This being is said, because of his human experience, to be responsible for the spiritual instruction of mankind, and as such appears on the earth when and where he wishes. Elijah is supposed to be one of his manifestations, as is Melchizedek (see p. 33). (Death turns away from Enoch, from ms. *Kosmas indikopleustes*, Sinai, 12th c.)

Solomon, the man who according to legend 'knew three Worlds', was a king with a deep understanding of esoteric matters. The possession of such knowledge bestows great occult powers, but does not always lead to the proper use of them. Despite his Wisdom (Hokhmah, on the Pillar of Force), Solomon became heedless of the constraint of the Pillar of Form, fell into a period of madness, and so lost his kingship and the inner connection of the spirit. Such a fall is possible even at the highest level of development. Wisdom does not always mean integrity: it requires the balance of Binah, Understanding. (Solomon and the Queen of Sheba, detail of fresco by Piero della Francesca, San Francesco, Arezzo, Italy, 15th c.)

Left:
Rabbi Akiba, who lived in first-century Palestine, was a mystic as well as a great scholar. He and his contemporary Rabbi Ishmael are cited in later Kabbalistic literature as men who ascended, in deep meditation, into the inner and upper Worlds and brought back accounts of what they had seen (see pp. 25–27). The practice of using famous names to give authority to an account by a later writer is not uncommon; the best known example is the Zohar, which has sections purportedly by Rabbi Simeon ben Yohai but probably written by the thirteenth-century Spanish Kabbalist Moses de Leon. (Rabbi Akiba, woodcut from Haggadah, Italy, 16th c.)

Next page, above:
Joshua ben Miriam of Nazareth is historically part of the Judaic line. His teaching, while cast in terms of allegory and action, has a very precise metaphysical background. We may never know whether he was trained by the Essenes or belonged to one of the many other mystical groups known to have existed in Palestine in his lifetime. Certainly he was a Master, if not – as the Christians maintain – the earthly manifestation of the spirit of the Messiah, the ideal human being who forms the hidden link between the highest Worlds and mankind. (Icon of Jesus with golden hair, Russia, 12th-13th c. Cathedral of the Assumption, Moscow.)

Right:
The coming of the Messiah has been a constant idea in Jewish history, and periodically, when the times have been calamitous, his arrival has been expected; according to tradition, such a moment is prophesied for redemption. Many pseudo-Messiahs, men of charismatic power and mystical knowledge, have arisen at such times. The last major case was in the seventeenth century, when Shabbetai Zvi attracted thousands of followers. His enforced conversion to Islam not only discredited him but led to rabbinical edicts restricting the study of Kabbalah to the mature, pious and learned. (Shabbetai Zvi, engraving from *The Counterfeit Messiah* by An English Person of Quality, 18th c.)

The arrival of the Messiah heralds the end of a Shemittah or cosmic cycle, when the spirits of the righteous are gathered together in the Holy Land – that is, the World of Beriah. Here Elijah precedes the Messiah into the celestial city. To the Kabbalist the Messiah is eternal: he was, is and shall be. His appearance in history signifies the moment when everyone must see in the perfect Adam the reflection of Divinity in the flesh. (Entry of the Messiah into Jerusalem, from Haggadah, Germany, 1753.)

Inner ascent

Ascent into the upper Worlds is the reward of individual merit, i.e. inner work; but there is also the phenomenon of Grace, as manifested in Jacob's experience at Bethel, where he was shown – while still spiritually asleep – a vision of the Ladder of Existence. Such a moment of awe confronts any individual with the decision whether to remain asleep below or to awake and consciously climb the ladder of evolution. (Jacob's dream, engraving from *Works* of John Milton, London, 1794–97.)

The quality of the inner Worlds is totally different from any earthly experience. From the outset, time and space take on unfamiliar values; nothing is substantial or solid; everything moves in an unfamiliar way. Forms take on a symbolic character, and events shift like a kaleidoscope. Here an artist conveys the otherworldliness of the realm in which angels and demons exist. The bridge marks the way through the chaos of lower Yezirah into the upper Worlds. Such interior journeys are highly perilous to the unprepared and may be undertaken only after much training. (The Bridge over Chaos, mezzotint by John Martin from *Paradise Lost* by John Milton, England, 19th c.)

Next page, above:
In the deepest and highest inner experiences, the mystic leaves the psychological realm of Yezirah, the World of Formation, and his consciousness enters Beriah, the World of Creation. Here, in spirit, he ascends to behold the Throne of Heaven, where his vision takes on a universal dimension. At this point between the cosmic and the Divine (see p. 15) is the place where the three upper Worlds meet; it is called the Seat of the Messiah, the dwelling of the most fully realized of human beings. Such a vision is granted to few, because it requires a great personal accumulation of merit and Divine Grace. (A mystic sees the Messiah surrounded by the four Holy Living Creatures, Apocalypse, Flanders, c. 1400. Bibliothèque Nationale, Paris.)

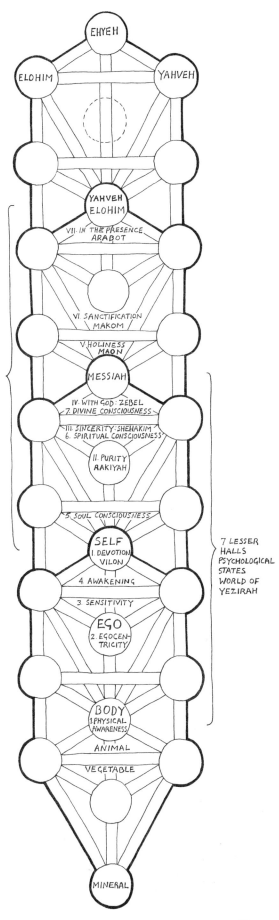

Right:

In Kabbalah there are two basic phases of ascent. The first, which belongs to the psychological World of Formation, is made up of seven levels, the Lesser Heikhalot or Halls. These are the steps by which one rises out of the midst of the body, through the lower psyche, into the level of the soul, and on to the spirit and the first contact with the Divine. The seven Greater Halls (or Heavens) mark successive levels of the spiritual World of Creation. The consciousness rises out of the psyche and through the lower levels of spirit, where the various Heavens are perceived as both states and stages of existence. The sixth and seventh Heavens are parallel to the lower parts of the Divine World of Emanation, and here the mystic may turn to come back, or go on to complete union with God. (Ladder of Greater and Lesser Halls.)

Diagram labels:

EHYEH

ELOHIM — YAHVEH

YAHVEH ELOHIM

VII. IN THE PRESENCE ARABOT

VI. SANCTIFICATION MAKOM

V. HOLINESS MAON

MESSIAH

IV. WITH GOD: ZEBEL — 7. DIVINE CONSCIOUSNESS

III. SINCERITY: SHEHAKIM — 6. SPIRITUAL CONSCIOUSNESS

II. PURITY RAKIYAH

5. SOUL CONSCIOUSNESS

SELF — I. DEVOTION VILON

4. AWAKENING

3. SENSITIVITY

EGO — 2. EGOCENTRICITY

BODY — 1. PHYSICAL AWARENESS

ANIMAL

VEGETABLE

MINERAL

VII GREATER HALLS: SPIRITUAL STATES WORLD OF BERIAH

7 LESSER HALLS PSYCHOLOGICAL STATES WORLD OF YEZIRAH

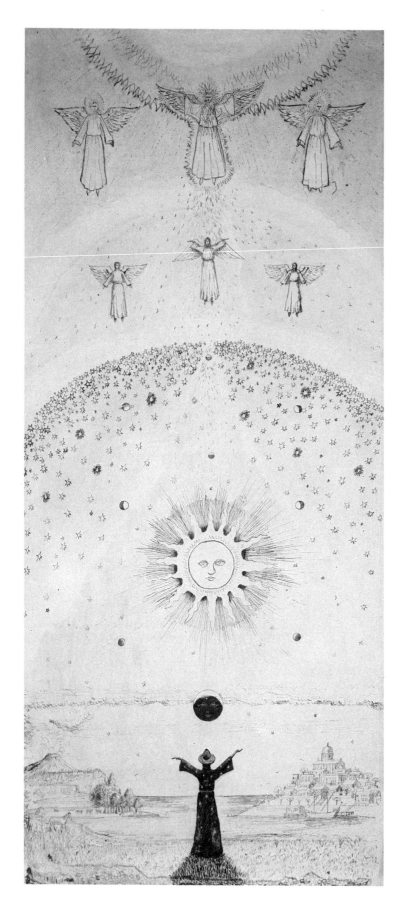

Work of Unification

The task of the Kabbalist, which under-lies all his work of personal development and all his visits to the higher regions, is to aid in the unification of the Worlds. As he brings unity into the four levels of his own being, he seeks to join that which is above to that which is below. In this picture a Kabbalist performs this act: he becomes conscious of the two uppermost Worlds and their inhabitants and draws the Divine Light down through the World of Formation – with its symbolic planetary archetypes arranged as a Sefirotic Tree – into himself and so to earth. (Kabbalist at work, screen. Author's Collection.)

Below:
The Work of Unification must involve contact with other spiritual traditions. At this level the outer forms of worship become less important: mystics meet in a spiritual World that is above form. A Jewish Kabbalist may converse with a Muslim Sufi or a Christian contemplative and discover the same reality beneath differing theories and practices. This unity at the spiritual level does not mean that the outer form of a tradition is redundant – each religion has its role to play – but that all human beings are made in the same Divine image. (The union of Islam, Christianity and Judaism, as figured by Rabbi Jacob Emden of Altona, Germany, 18th c.)

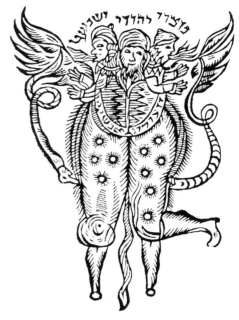

Right:

The construction of the tabernacle, as given in Exodus 25–27, is a symbol of all the Worlds. The hierarchical organization of the Hebrews reflects the truth that everyone has a place in the arrangement of existence; and in an act of communal worship every level participates in the Work of Unification. To the Kabbalist this view of the tabernacle reveals in detail the various stages of spirituality. Such an example is typical of the depths found within a biblical text. (The symbolism of the tabernacle, set out on Jacob's Ladder, after Halevi, *Kabbalah and Exodus.* See p. 70.)

Below:

Unification is carried out in action, in devotion, and in contemplation. Here a prayer is written out in the figure of a man who wears a crown. Thus, while the Kabbalist prays, he becomes aware of the head, body and limbs both of himself and of Adam Kadmon, the primordial man (see p. 68). He shifts his consciousness from the personal to the Divine, thereby bringing himself into union with Adam Kadmon, of whom he is a reflection, and who is in turn the reflection of the Divine. Thus a human individual aids God to behold God. (Divine image in prayer from ms. Hebrew prayer book, France or Germany, 13th–14th c. British Library, London.)

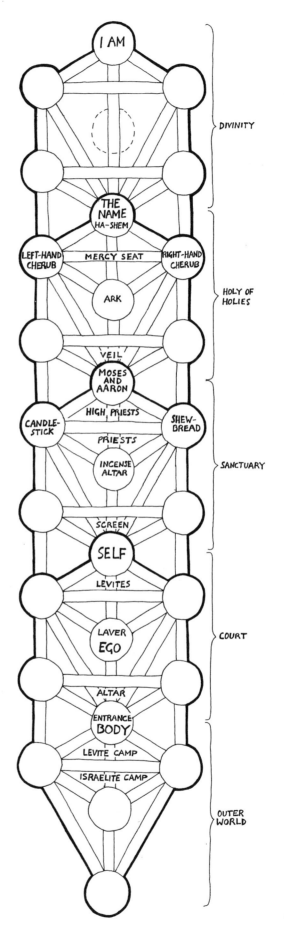

The End of Days

In each of the seven universal cycles of Creation, or Shemittot, the impulse of Divine consciousness passes down from Beriah, the World of Creation, through a Sefirotic chain into full manifestation in matter and rises again, full of experience, into the World of Creation. On the final day of the last Shemittah it arrives at its penultimate stage. On this day every being that has been called forth, created, formed and made is assessed according to its performance throughout time and is sent to its rightful place in Creation. After this, all are merged in the World of Emanation, the being of Adam Kadmon. (Last Judgment, engraving by Gustave Doré, France, 19th c.)

When Adam Kadmon has absorbed and realized all the experience of everything that has been brought into being, then the image of the Divine knows Who is within and without. In this mirror, Face gazes upon Face, and total union occurs. Then I AM THAT I AM is One, and existence vanishes, leaving God alone. God has beheld God. (The Holy Name EHYEH ASHER EHYEH, I AM THAT I AM, calligraphy. Joseph Russell Collection, New York.)

Further reading

Blumenthal, David, *Understanding Jewish Mysticism: A Source Reader*, Ktav, New York 1978.

Charles, R.H., *et al.* (eds), *Apocrypha and Pseudepigrapha of the Old Testament in English*, 2 vols, OUP, Oxford 1963.

Cordovero, Moses ben J., *The Palm Tree of Deborah* (ed. and trs. from the Hebrew by L. Jacobs), Vallentine, Mitchell, London 1960; Sepher-Hermon Press, New York 1974.

Dobh Baer, Rabbi Ben Schneor, *Tract on Ecstasy* (trs. from the Hebrew by L. Jacobs), Vallentine, Mitchell, London 1963.

Encyclopaedia Judaica (eds in chief: C. Roth, G. Wigoder, *et al.*), 16 vols, Jerusalem, and Macmillan, New York 1971, 1972.

Encyclopaedia of the Jewish Religion (eds: R. J. Zwi Werblowski, G. Wigoder), Holt, Rinehart & Winston, New York 1966; Phoenix, London 1967.

Epstein, Perle, *Kabbalah: Way of the Jewish Mystic*, Doubleday, New York 1978.

Franck, Adolphe, *The Kabbalah: the Religious Philosophy of the Hebrews* (trs from the French), University Books, New York 1967.

Ginsburg, Christian D., *The Kabbalah: The Essenes*, Routledge & Kegan Paul, London 1968; Weiser, New York 1970.

Halevi, Z'ev ben Shimon, *A Kabbalistic Universe*, Rider, London, and Weiser, New York 1977.

——, *Adam and the Kabbalistic Tree*, Rider, London, and Weiser, New York 1974.

——, *Kabbalah and Exodus*, Rider, London, and Weiser, New York (in preparation).

——, *The Way of Kabbalah*, Rider, London, and Weiser, New York 1976.

——, *Tree of Life: an Introduction to the Cabala*, Rider, London, and Weiser, New York 1972.

Jacobs, Louis, *A Jewish Theology*, Darton, Longman & Todd, London 1973; Behrmann House, New York 1974.

——, *Hasidic Prayer*, Routledge & Kegan Paul, London 1972; Schocken Books, New York 1973.

——, *Jewish Mystical Testimonies*, Schocken Books, New York 1976.

——, *Seeker of Unity: the Life and Works of Aaron of Starosselje*, Basic Books, New York and Vallentine, Mitchell, London 1966.

Jewish Encyclopedia (reprint of 1904 edn, ed. I. Singer), 12 vols, Ktav, New York 1964.

Kenton, Warren, *The Anatomy of Fate*, Rider, London, and Weiser, New York 1978.

Krakowsky, Rabbi, *Kabbalah, Light of Redemption*, Research Center of Kabbalah, Jerusalem and New York 1970.

Mathers, S.L.M. (ed. and trs.), *Kabbalah Unveiled: Books of the Zohar* (reprint of 1900 edn, trs. from the Latin of K. von Rosenroth), Routledge & Kegan Paul, London 1970; Weiser, New York 1970.

Meltzer, David (ed.), *Secret Garden: an Anthology in the Kabbalah*, Seabury Press, New York 1976.

Müller, Ernst, *History of Jewish Mysticism*, Phaidon Press, Oxford 1946; Yesod, New York 1978.

Myer, Isaac, *Qabbalah. The Philosophical Writings of Solomon Ben Yehudah Ibn Gebirol* (reprint of 1888 edn), 2nd edn, Weiser, New York, and Stuart & Watkins, London 1970.

Rosenberg, Roy A. (trs.), *Anatomy of God: Book of Concealment*, Ktav, New York 1973.

Schaya, Leo, *The Universal Meaning of the Kaballah* (trs. from the French by N. Pearson), Allen & Unwin, London 1971; University Books, Secaucus 1972.

Scholem, Gershom, *Kabbalah*, Keter, Jerusalem, and New York Times Book Co., New York 1974.

——, *Kabbalah and its Symbolism*, Routledge & Kegan Paul, London 1975.

——, *Major Trends in Jewish Mysticism*, Thames & Hudson, London 1955; Schocken Books, New York 1974.

——, *Zohar, Book of Splendor: Basic Readings from the Kabbalah*, Schocken Books, New York 1963; Rider, London 1977.

Sepher Yezirah (reprint of 1877 edn, trs. from the Hebrew by F. Kalisch), AMORC, San José 1972.

3 Enoch or, the Hebrew Book of Enoch (trs. from the Hebrew by H. Odeberg), CUP, Cambridge 1928; Ktav, New York 1973.

Waite, A.E., *Holy Kabbalah: A Study of the Secret Tradition*, University Books, New York 1972.

Weiner, Herbert, $9\frac{1}{2}$ *Mystics: the Kabbala Today*, Holt, Rinehart & Winston, New York and Chicago 1969.

Werblowsky, R. J. Zwi, *Joseph Karo, Lawyer and Mystic*, OUP, Oxford 1978; Jewish Publication Society of America, Philadelphia 1976.

Zalman, Rabbi Schneor, *Philosophy of Chabad*, Chabad Research Center, New York 1973.

Zohar (trs. from the Aramaic by H. Sperling, M. Simon and P.P. Lavertoff), Soncino Press, London 1931–34.

Acknowledgments

The objects shown in the plates, pp. 33–64, are in the collections of:
Aachen, Suermondt-Ludwig-Museum 63; Amsterdam, Rijksmuseum 51 a; Bamberg, State Library 60; Berlin (West), Gemäldegalerie 51 e, f; Copenhagen, National Library 57; Dublin, National Gallery of Ireland 51 g; Ein Harod, Museum of Art 58 below; Florence, Biblioteca Nazionale 53; Jerusalem, Schocken Institute 52; Leningrad, The Hermitage 51 b; London, British Library 34, 36, Jewish Museum 55, 62, Warren Kenton 38, 39, 64, National Gallery 51 d, j, Victoria and Albert Museum, 42; New York, Jewish Museum 58 above, Jewish Theological Seminary of America 58–59, Metropolitan Museum of Art 43, Joseph Russell 38, 64; Paris Louvre, 51 h; Rotterdam, Boymans-van Beuningen Museum 50 c; Sarajevo Museum 61; Stockholm, Nationalmuseum 50 i; Tel Aviv, Einhorn Collection 56; Vienna, Akademie der Bildenden Künste 46; Österreichische Galerie 48–49.

Photographs were made available by:
PLATES British Library 34, 36; J. R. Freeman 55; Giraudon 51 h; David Harris 52; Ann Münchow 63; Palphot 44–45; Picturepoint 33; Scala 53; Eileen Tweedy 42, 64; Warburg Institute 62. THEMES Biblioteca Ambrosiana 78 above; British Library 80 top r., 85 top l., 86 below; J. R. Freeman 66 above; Gabinetto Fotografico Nazionale 75 below; Giraudon 71 above; David Harris 80 below l.; Israel Tourist Office 81 above; Jewish National University Library 65, 68 below l., 70 above, 80 below r., 82 r.; Mansell Collection 71 below, 88 centre; Radio Times Hulton Picture Library 86 above; United Grand Lodge of England 79 below l.; Warburg Institute 70 below r., 80 above l., 83 above r.